About the

Gabriella Bellairs-Lombard (Gabi) has been writing a collection of short stories and letters since she was young, about events she imagined or experienced. At the age of twelve, she left Johannesburg with her family for Riyadh, Saudi Arabia, and lived there for four years, attending the British International School in Riyadh. At the age of sixteen, she completed her schooling at Malvern College in the United Kingdom and returned home to South Africa to study a Bachelor of Journalism from Rhodes University. Upon graduating she entered the working world, specialising in various forms of marketing, but predominantly in copywriting.

Gabi has been a passionate writer for as long as she can remember, transferring her love for words to her career as she started her own freelance business and working remotely for companies overseas. She conducts all her work from her home office in the KwaZulu-Natal Midlands. She is often distracted by her family members, dogs and a sixteen-year-old Maine Coon cat, and is a huge advocate for mental health, animal rights and gender equality.

FINDING FOREVER: CHRONICLES OF AN EXPAT TEENAGER

Gabriella Bellairs-Lombard

FINDING FOREVER: CHRONICLES OF AN EXPAT TEENAGER

Vanguard Press

A CIP catalogue record for this title is
available from the British Library.

ISBN 978-1-80016-084-2

*Vanguard Press is an imprint of
Pegasus Elliot MacKenzie Publishers Ltd.*
www.pegasuspublishers.com

First Published in 2021

**Vanguard Press
Sheraton House Castle Park
Cambridge England**

Printed & Bound in Great Britain

Dedication

To my family:
In the name of patience and perseverance.

                                    – our family motto

'Write what disturbs you, what you fear, what you have
not been willing to speak about. Be willing to be split
open.'

                                    – Natalie Goldberg
                    Wild Mind: Living the Writer's Life (2011)

Acknowledgements

To my mom and dad: thank you for supporting my brave plan to write a book, even at the tender age of fourteen Your guidance in all aspects of my life has led me to where I am and is the reason why you two are the first to be mentioned on this page. What you don't realise is that I drew much of my inspiration and strength from the examples you have both set my entire life. Thank you for being excited about my dreams and for your patience when I opt for a nap instead of executing said dreams. I love you both so much.

To my sister, Kate: thank you for making me laugh so much and for being my partner in mischief; for your extraordinary insights and encouragement when things feel icky (and for telling me to 'suck it up' when I'm being a wet); for being my lifelong singing partner even though only one of us can sing; and for being my best friend throughout it all. You are so special, and I love you very much.

To my family: thank you, Granny and Grandpa, for always supporting and loving my writing, and for your many book vouchers that have afforded me books that have made me a better writer. You both mean the world to me—thank you for making me smile so often. To Nana and Tony, thank you for being ever-present and for being like my personal fans. I hope you know I am a *huge* fan of you both, too. Janene and Roger, you epitomise strength and resilience in times of adversity. Thank you for being so loving and invested in my life. Bobby, Andy, Amy and Nic—you are forces to be reckoned with. Thank you for your support always. To my cousins, Dev and Dane, you are fearless and two of my best friends and I am infinitely thankful for your never-ending support and love. Drinking fantastic red wine with you is one of my favourite pastimes.

To John: your support never goes unnoticed. You have helped me become better in so many ways and I will never stop thanking you for all that you do, including your support of me completing this book. You are incredibly special, and I am so excited to see what life has in store for us. Thank you for all our fun memories—I love you, my 'tato!

To my friends: Jess White and Abbie Daniels, my two comrades in life who I would be nothing without—thank you for being my best friends, for being my drinking buddies when I needed you, for your honesty and for your commitment to our friendship always. I know that when life feels uncertain, one certainty will remain—and that is that I have both of you. Thank you for everything. To my friends in Johannesburg, the Midlands and everywhere in between: you have been the glue that held everything together. Thank you for being my support system and for cheering me on. You all know who you are.

To my editor, Brenda Nieburg: choosing you as my editor is one of the greatest decisions I've ever made; you'll know this is true because you've read my book and know how many questionable decisions I have made in my life. Thank you for helping me to write my best work and for being so supportive along the way— you and I were the perfect match and I now consider you a dear friend. I can't wait for us to work together again soon.

To my teachers: you have all shaped me into who I am, and I am forever grateful for your guidance and encouragement. This book wouldn't have come to life if it weren't for you.

To my Saudi family: this book is because of you. Whether you're near or far, in touch with me or not, you shaped my experiences in Saudi in the most special way and this will never be taken away from me. Thank you for the various roles you played, and still play, in my life.

INTRODUCTION

How on earth am I supposed to begin describing how this book came about?

I'll start at the most obvious point. I went to the Kingdom of Saudi Arabia at the age of twelve. I left when I was just over fifteen. I decided I needed to write about it. End.

No, but that's not just it. This book is like that foster puppy that has been to many homes but somehow always ends up back at the pound—he's not cute enough, he's too needy, or he's not even a puppy any more so has lost his appeal. But now, the puppy (who is now an adult dog) has found a loving home of dog-lovers (like the obsessed, crazy dog ladies I see in my family) who have no intention of letting him go. He is home, finally.

This book has also finally come home. It is complete; it no longer needs attention to detail or content, and its wholesome honesty is evergreen.

It started when I simply had a story to share.

Are there any teenage, white, female expats who have written about their experiences in the Middle East? I asked myself. *Well, not that I know of.*

So, I set about earnestly trying to tell my tale, which I thought would fill a gap in the world of stories and, while it starts as 'my' story, it subsequently became the story of many other girls who faced the same kinds of battles, joys, and learning curves as I did.

This book has undergone a multitude of surgeries to make it what it is now. Revision after revision, edit after edit, failure after failure. I have ripped it apart and stitched it back together again, trying not to lose its heartbeat throughout, but my book has made it out alive and I present it to you now in its truest form.

You might ask how you can trust a story that was conceived when I was fifteen and is only being completed at the age of twenty-five? I understand why. Memory is the greatest and most unreliable thing there is when it comes to telling a story. But this story is more than just a retelling of events, even though I am only sharing them now. It's about a young girl's bravery in overcoming things that shouldn't have happened to her, and about the difficulties of navigating adolescence in a country that wasn't hers and was defined by an amalgamation of different cultures and ideals. Part of the process of writing this book was revisiting both painful and positive events and experiences, which involved a huge amount of introspection, and deciding if writing about them would benefit both myself and the reader. There's universality to some of my stories, and I ask you to trust in this.

Whether you believe it or not, though, is your prerogative. I am here to let you in on a world that was mine for a very significant period in my life. And maybe it will resonate with you, maybe it won't. But a big part of writing this book was to take ownership of an experience that changed my life forever.

So, welcome, and enjoy the journey.

CHAPTER ONE
Finding my feet

Saudi Arabia's nickname was 'the Land of Sand' and I have never known a phrase to be more literal. This was the place from which I drew enough inspiration to start this book. You may view this book as an accessible diary of a period in a person's life, or you may view this as commentary on what it was like to be a white, female teenager living in Saudi Arabia. Either way, this book is the physical representation of my life's events for a period of time.

It wasn't just any country awaiting our arrival. In April 2007, I departed the comfort of my Johannesburg bubble and jetted off to Riyadh, Saudi Arabia—Riyadh being the capital of Saudi, and Saudi the Muslim capital of the world. My dad went ahead of us to start his new job; my mom, sister and I followed shortly after. My mom was holding us all together quite stoically—she knew she would be fine as long as she had her family and her dogs. But what was hanging in the air at that point was how she was going to survive without a bottle store for her nightly glass of wine and maybe-more-than-one-glass-and-a-gin on the weekends.

Oops, I just made my mom sound like an alcoholic.

Let me clarify: alcohol is illegal in Saudi Arabia. There is literally no negotiation allowed on this issue. Alcohol is not something my family uses to cope—a glass of wine is like the full stop at the end of the day, indicating that 'yes, you may relax now and stop thinking about the worries of the day'. It is sociable and brings people together and has always been something positive.

Mom was graceful. Sister (Kate) was too young to know what was really going on but was a little nervous. I was freaking fuming.

How dare they take me away from my happy life? I'm twelve now, I have a boyfriend who plays soccer with me whenever I want to (but he'd better not even *try* to hold my hand); I have the most perfect group of friends; everyone in my grade loves me; and I am on the cusp of making the A team for soccer. And now I must leave all of this behind to go to a freaking sandpit. I am so incredibly angry. This is so unfair, Mom and Dad. *So. Unfair.*

***

I had the usual farewell at school. When someone leaves, everyone signs their shirt with cute little messages about how cool they are and how much they will be missed. I had two of these shirts because I couldn't get enough of the attention. I also couldn't get enough of the memories I so badly wanted to take with me, whether in physical form or just those that resided in my head. I was shattered—absolutely broken that my life of comfort, happiness, friendship, love and attachment had been torn apart by a move that was centred around a job. *Was our current life not enough?* I struggled to see beyond my own two feet or what the end goal was here.

We sold our house, the one I was born in and grew up in for twelve years—the first of many incredibly painful moves. We moved to a poky little townhouse just up the road that would be our 'lock up and go' home when we came back for visits. I had to share a bunk bed with my sister and the tumble dryer was in my study room.

So, we must live like sardines and then move to a country that is ninety percent sand? How is this 'for the benefit of our family'?

The reality was something I would only later understand. The reality was that this really was for the benefit of our family. But I had no idea what our lives would turn into upon arriving at Riyadh airport.

It's safe to say that one's welcome to the country is far from glamorous. The beginning, though, definitely was—my dad's new bank paid for first class tickets for all of us to ensure maximum comfort. I hadn't even smelled first class, let alone sat in one of the seats. I was a bit suspicious, like they were trying to buy our loyalty to their country, but I certainly didn't complain when the air hostesses were making a bed for me on the aeroplane, and nor did my mom, who was sipping on a glass of French champagne topped up by attentive hostesses.

Approaching Riyadh was so disappointing; I was expecting a bustling night scene with lots of lights and tall buildings but, no, it really was just a large expanse of sand. So, its nickname was true, then.

The airport looked like an ugly wedding cake and the people inside it were unfriendly, and I couldn't see their faces because of their black and white robes and headscarf things.

Where on Earth have my parents brought me?

I couldn't imagine how I was going to be happy in a place where a woman's physical appearance was limited to just her eyes, where the men did not shy away from staring, and where people from places like India, Pakistan and Sri Lanka, in Riyadh as basic labourers so that they could support their families, were pushed together like dominoes and spoken to as though they were sub-human. I have never felt so uncertain of the future as I did in that line to check our passports. I was wide-eyed and bushy-tailed, but without the bushy tail.

Walking through that airport I realised how I was going to feel over the next three years: like a visitor.

Our trip to Saudi made me realise how small my world was previously. I had my routines and familiar faces and spaces, and nothing monumental ever disturbed that. Then I arrived in Dubai to connect to Riyadh, and I didn't know what to do with myself. It was *huge* and there were cool-looking gadgets everywhere.

I often thought: *Someone lives a life like this and it's completely normal for them. Yet, here I am, open-mouthed at the seven iPods in front of me, and a shop full of perfumes I have never even heard of.*

The meaning of 'normal' started to change, but was this a good or bad thing? South Africa, the world I knew so well, was not like this.

How was I going to adapt?

***

The story of why we moved to Saudi is pretty easy to understand. My dad was in the banking industry—corporate banking, to be specific—and had worked for several banks in South Africa, including the likes of Standard Bank and Barclays Africa. He had worked for his boss for about ten years, a large, kind Brazilian man who had relocated to Saudi to start a new job in the banking sector. Their strong relationship was a well-balanced combination of friendship and business, going on several hunting trips together over the years, and he wanted my dad to join him in Riyadh. A job offer came, as expected, and we knew that the opportunities that came with this offer were almost impossible to ignore.

The reality of being a white, older male working in South Africa was beginning to rear its head. There was very little, or no, room for growth, and the desire to succeed in an environment that constantly overlooked people like my dad was becoming overwhelming. With income taxes eating away at possibilities for us as a family, the thought of earning a tax-free income in Saudi had immense appeal. At the forefront of this was the knowledge that my parents could eventually afford superior education for their children now that this opportunity had been presented. I was twelve when I left South Africa, my sister was nine; we were at a good age to have some long-term change injected into our lives, even though I could not anticipate what was coming.

My attitude to the move was compulsively negative. The thought of leaving my best friends and my country inspired a deeply embedded feeling of bitterness in me. Maturity had not set in yet—I had never dealt with such an emotionally charged situation before—so I took it out on my family. As much as my parents reassured me that South Africa would always be our home and that we would be back someday, I couldn't look past what was happening. Things were going so well for me (as well as they could at the ripe old age of twelve), and it felt like that was all being taken away. I quite simply was only thinking about myself.

Eventually, I started seeing some light at the end of this sandy tunnel. That feeling of bitterness gradually faded as I slowly started to look forward to a new beginning. My dad signed his work contract, which was set to last for three years and was later extended to five. The nature of job contracts in Saudi was a strange one because no one ever arrived when they were supposed to or left when they were supposed to. Things were always changing, and never on your terms. This was one of the characteristics of life in Saudi: things were *always* changing, but they were always changing *for you* with very little acknowledgement of your concerns or circumstances. You would always be a puppet as long as you remained in the country.

***

We were dubbed 'Westerners' in this foreign land, and did not have a free choice regarding where we wanted to live upon arrival. Our 'home' during our time here was allocated to us. One of the consequences of moving to a country like Saudi—just to make sure it is completely alien to the rest of the world and that Westerners have as little control as possible—is that we were forbidden to be involved in real estate.

In place of this, we lived in 'compounds': a collection of living quarters enclosed by a really high wall. I described them as similar to luxurious refugee camps for anyone who isn't native to Saudi Arabia. Westerners were housed completely separately from Arabs. We lived in our world and the Arabs in theirs, as two pockets of people totally unique in themselves.

We moved into a compound called Eid Villas. The first time I set eyes on the place, I wasn't sure if I could ever get used to what I saw becoming a part of my everyday life. From the moment we approached the first entrance, I had an inkling of the extent to which we were going to be protected. The first gate was bulletproof, with a little guardhouse and waiting room. After that came a sheltered search point where every inch of your vehicle is inspected, including the underside. As a naïve young girl who always thought the best of everyone, I asked myself who would either want, or be dumb enough, to attempt smuggling some form of contraband, presumably weaponry, into the compound. But it turned out that these things were actual possibilities and had to be considered when controlling the flow of people (either residents or guests) in and out of the compounds. This was standard procedure for compounds all around Riyadh.

Once the vehicle inspection was done, you drove past a military tank—Saudi National Guards—then another tank after navigating your way around strategically placed concrete bollards, designed specifically to slow your vehicle down. Finally, you arrived at the official entrance to the compound after presenting your Iqama, which is your resident's ID, or your passport. If you were a visitor, both of these were vital to allow you into the compound.

I was in awe. For a moment I forgot about the fact that I had just left behind twelve years of memories and friends and focused my attention on my new home for the next three years. There were extravagantly lit fountains and palm trees, a recreational centre, a massive wave pool with a twirly-whirly slide, all to create this perception of luxury and comfort that a normal Western world would offer. Ironically, considering the country I was now in, the amount of freedom I could sense in this little piece of paradise was overwhelming.

You may or may not be asking why such stringent security measures were in place on the borders of the compound. In 2003, the hearts and minds of people in the city were struck when three compounds were bombed. Discrimination did not come into play— everyone was affected in one way or another. It undeniably made a small mark on the country's history, and most certainly shook the city of Riyadh forever. One evening in May of that year, while the majority of all Western compounds were innocently sleeping, four vehicles drove through Riyadh, carrying heavily armed assault teams and dangerous explosives, and proceeded to destroy homes and lives. Because I was not in the country at that time, I relied on the stories of those who were, and I pictured myself being just as terrified as they were.

Lives, homes, safety and hope were all lost. After the bombing, hundreds of Western wives and children fled the country in an attempt to find somewhere bomb-free to carry on with schooling. A few came back once they knew the country was safer again.

Al-Hamra compound had previously been built onto the British International School of Riyadh (BISR)—which was the school I attended—and was one of the main compounds targeted. When we arrived at the school it was on the verge of closing down due to the lack of students, everyone leaving the country, as well as some family members who feared for their personal safety. In the end, they had to start accepting non-British passport holders in a desperate attempt to get the school running again, which was partially the reason for the large Arab influence in the school by the time I got there.

I asked a form teacher, Mr Bull, to tell me his version of events. The detailed way in which he told the story of how he had to hide in his bathroom while the rest of his house was bombed almost placed me there with him. He could have died, and I saw the fear flash across his face once again. I couldn't imagine his life being restored to normality after that, when his home and faith and humour had been destroyed. Another friend told me that he had to run out of his house in his undies, with his younger brother, and hide under a mattress.

All the while I was thinking: *Well, we had a video camera stolen once.*

Security in Riyadh was elevated to a different level after that tragic event. The country was always prepared from then on.

Being inside a compound was exciting and liberating, sheltered from the drama outside its borders. My house, Villa 190, was within close range of all activity: it was across the road from the supermarket (which I frequented for Bounty chocolate bars, Baskin Robbins ice cream and chewing gum), wave pool and recreation centre, and behind my house was one of four satellite pools, a basketball court and tennis courts. I definitely thought life could get worse than what it was at the time.

The compound came alive over weekends; I lived for these. I just had to first get used to the fact that my week started on a Saturday and ended on a Wednesday. I could not wrap my head around this bizarre system initially, even though I knew it was because Fridays are like the Christian Sunday to the Islamic community and, oh yes, I was currently living in the most Islamic country in the world.

My Johannesburg world expanded again when I became integrated into an international group of people. I remember looking out of my bedroom window once and seeing a group of girls talking in the streets and saying to myself in excitement, "Oh my gosh, Americans!" The basketball court behind my house had been transformed into a street court for kids to play soccer, each one of them taking the game as seriously as their limitations would allow. I would soon be one of them.

I was incredibly shy in the beginning and wasn't quite sure how to put myself out there—it was intimidating knowing I had been thrown into a pool of international people and I had no idea how to swim. But one night, from my back door, as I timidly watched people playing soccer on the basketball court, I grabbed a chair and moved closer, and just sat there and observed. In hindsight this was pretty creepy, but a young girl with long, black hair named Phoebe came up to me and asked if I wanted to play. Young Gabi took this opportunity to meet the people she had been ogling from her bedroom window (again, creepy). I played soccer with them for around three hours that night and even developed a small crush on a blond Belgian boy, who was a bit older than me. The diversity and sense of freedom amongst these kids inspired a different sense of 'carefree' in me, and I was beyond excited to be able to act on it.

The friends that I made on the compound later turned into a form of family for me. There was a Brazilian-German boy with short, curly hair who flaunted every piece of FC Barcelona apparel possible most days and was a clown that everyone adored. Not the sharpest tool in the shed, but he was a ball to be around, and Eid Compound was pretty much his own family, too. I don't think he had much family life at home.

The compound manager's son—a boy my age from Egypt that everyone seemed to pick on—was often by his side. Amongst the Arabs and other people who had been in Saudi for a long time, there appeared to be an on-going joke regarding Egyptians, which I didn't really understand but chose to laugh about, too. This boy seemed to thrive on irritating people, but he had one of the biggest hearts. He always put other people ahead of himself and never missed a chance to play soccer or hang out with us, even though he was the go-to person when someone needed a last-minute sign-in of a friend, purely because he was the manager's son. As the years went on, he never seemed to grow older. He was like our child that we could never get rid of, but would feel the difference if he wasn't around.

Our little group was made up of nationalities from all around the world. South Africans (mainly just me but a few others came and went), Germans, Brazilians, Egyptians, Belgians, Americans, Lebanese, Argentinians... all people completely foreign to my little bubble in Johannesburg, and all of whom had a massive impact on my life. They were all of the 'international' state of mind: open-minded, experienced and full of knowledge, and ultimately appeared a lot more mature than me. I later became one of these people after travelling to many countries and broadening my cultural lens.

Sometimes things got boring in the compound, so we often resorted to crazy activities, like climbing the emergency ladders onto the tops of the roofs and playing 'ding-dong-ditch'. I became best friends with an

American-Puerto Rican girl named Ashleigh who was my age and was always up for doing absolutely anything with me. One evening we were bored, as explained, and decided to 'ding-dong-ditch' her bus monitor. She was a rather intolerant Pakistani lady with a distinct accent, yet she insisted on telling people she was from Chicago. We might've taken our game a bit too far, to the point where either she or her daughter would wait for us to ring their doorbell and then chase after us. One of the younger girls we knew, who was about eleven years old, decided to follow our lead and play the game herself, but unfortunately came off short. As she was about to ring the bell, the woman stormed out of the house and slapped this kid across the face. Ashleigh's mom got involved and, of course, there was a pile of denial from the other side. It's safe to say that we learned our lesson, both about knowing when to stop, and setting an example for those younger than us.

I started playing soccer when I was eight years old, and by the time I had left South Africa, I felt like a skilled and confident player. Soccer very quickly became an obsession. The year after we arrived in Riyadh, a half-sized soccer pitch was built in our compound and little did I know that it would be there that most of my soccer skill and passion would be born. I had more time to teach myself tricks and techniques, and I was absorbing the talent that surrounded me. I developed my own mini-idols of people in the compound that I really looked up to and admired. One was a Danish boy who was older than me but a wizard with the ball (although he had a slight temper on the field), and the other was the cute Belgian boy I was crushing on, who controlled the ball like it was his own. Younger Gabi only wanted to be like them with a soccer ball.

***

I went through a bit of a phase, like any teenager does, I think; except mine involved being the victim of excessive bullying, and I quickly became a walkover, a doormat for everyone to wipe their dirty feet on. I hadn't the slightest clue how to stand up for myself because, in my naïve head, we didn't do that in South Africa. Just like meeting people of different nationalities was new, as was living in a compound, getting bullied was new, too. I had never experienced conflict (except for one small fight in grade four over an Economics and Management Sciences project) in my perfect life. In Saudi, I tended to forgive people far too quickly for them to learn to respect me. After being molly-coddled and loved by everyone and loving everyone in return at my comfortable private school in Johannesburg, this was a bit of an eye-opener. I was never taught how to defend myself.

A boy from Pretoria moved into the compound, and I was over-the-moon excited to have another South African hang out with us. Things didn't go as planned

31

and he later turned into the very first person in my life that I ever hated. He was Afrikaans, from an Afrikaans family; I left South Africa too soon to know how to speak any Afrikaans. He was older, bigger, and had a tendency to pick on those much smaller than him.

The one time I stood up to him he snapped back venomously, "Shut up! And stop thinking you're a proper South African when you can't even speak Afrikaans."

Being the little patriot I was, I was incredibly hurt by this. To hear someone else, never mind another South African, insult me about my origins was offensive because living away from home had made me prouder than ever to be South African. How dare this moron make me feel like none of that was even real? As most things go in life, you have to get hurt like that by people like him to know who is worth your time, even if you were the last two South Africans left on Earth.

The compounds may have had massive boundary walls and fences, but living inside felt like we were roaming free—free of limits, even some rules. My parents could drink in the compound and no one could say anything: compounds were like micro countries with their own regulations. One of the things most concerning for a family who grew up with evening drinks and many beers on the weekends was that we couldn't freely go to buy alcohol.

A recipe to make wine was passed on to us, which only required wine yeast (kindly gifted to us by a

Zimbabwean lady in our compound) and white grape juice. Shortly after this my mom arrived home with litres of Ceres white grape juice. We filled a bottle from the water dispenser with grape juice and yeast, assembled the funnel and completed the process with a condom to measure when the yeast had fermented. (At the time, much to my dismay, I discovered my dad frantically searching for something. When I asked what he was looking for, he replied, "I'm looking for a damn condom." Imagine my confusion, as I knew that my mom had undergone a hysterectomy a few years previously. I also would come close to nausea and hysteria thinking of my parents doing the hanky-panky.)

Other than our trusty home brew, which my mom swore was magic juice (and so did others, as many were interested in buying it from her)—it didn't get you too drunk and didn't give you a hangover because there were none of the added sulphates and other chemicals found in a normal bottle of wine—my dad experimented with the black market. He bought whisky that cost two hundred dollars a bottle, but this was all in a desperate attempt to try to make things feel normal, even if this version of normal seemed slightly synthetic. We learnt to make the best of our situation; we could only be as happy as we wanted to be.

I completely took advantage of an empty house when my parents were out. The whole 'roaming free' thing was taken to another level when I had the house, and the booze cupboard, to myself. When I was fourteen there was one night when my boyfriend at the time, Ashleigh, and I, were home alone. I had been eyeing the cupboard with the homemade vodka in it. We drank shots of it and made cocktails (as best as we could at fourteen) and ultimately got completely and utterly sozzled. Homemade vodka does not go through the same filtering processes as proper vodka, so it was essentially like drinking pure ethanol that burnt the inside of your soul, and really should not be messed with the way we did. That night, I face-planted on a speed bump, vomited my lungs out, and could not even sit on the couch without falling off. I was grounded for a month when my parents came home later to find me passed out in bed.

***

I have made it sound like drinking was something you could get away with. Take your drinking habits beyond the borders of the compound and you were stepping on incredibly dangerous territory. The Saudis may be backward and irrational and ridiculous, according to my young eyes at the time, but they had the power to decide whether or not you may stay in their country.

With just the slightest hint of alcohol on your breath, you would be packing your bags quicker than you could say, "I swear to drunk, Officer, I'm not God." No negotiation, no joking around, no bribing (sorry,

Saffers*[1]). This happened to two people I knew at the time. It's difficult to wrap your head around being punished for something that was always part of your normal life, but not theirs. You very quickly became accustomed to, and accepted, Saudi's strange ways of living: you made your own alcohol and made sure none of it left your house; you ate beef bacon instead of pork; and you definitely didn't call your wife to fetch you after a heavy night at the embassy. Mind you, driving for women was illegal back then, so I guess you couldn't do that, either.

Somehow—and this is probably because I had difficulty saying no and people took advantage of this—my house became the place to be when parents were away, and kids were bored. Even though my house was left in a state not unlike a war zone, we made some incredible memories. Those memories made that house my home for the time I was there.

Compounds are essentially like really big cliques, some of which have bad reputations. Thankfully, Eid had a great reputation. Cordoba compound was one of the popular ones but apparently it was also where the youth went to dabble in marijuana and other varieties of home brew. All the British Aerospace Engineering (BAE) and Ministry of Defence (MOD) families lived in Salwa compound, also warmly known as the 'white' compound by the Arab people I knew. Salwa had the

*[1] Saffers: A nickname given to South Africans.

lead on cool compounds because it had proper bars, and families were given alcohol with their salaries. I went there quite often due to the large number of my English friends, including a boyfriend. They took normal to a whole new level, where I sometimes managed to forget I was in Saudi.

***

Speaking of rules and regulations, one had to question the judicial system in Saudi when people were deported for having alcohol in their cars—a normal situation for those from Western countries—and others were allowed to get away with harassing women, for example.

However, there was always 'Chop Chop' Square to sort people out. Formally known as Deera Square, this area in Riyadh was cleared by Saudi police each week after Friday prayers for executions to take place. If you raped or murdered, you were beheaded. If you were caught stealing multiple times, your arm was chopped off, hence the nickname. You'd think, with these consequences pretty much set, in stone, that locals would steer clear of committing any kind of crime. Like anywhere else in the world, crime happened in Saudi regardless of the known consequences.

Unfortunately, we were some of the unlucky few victims of crime in Riyadh. My dad had just started out in Riyadh—we hadn't arrived yet—and had to run an errand in the centre of the city (very different to the Johannesburg CBD). He had left his briefcase under the front passenger seat of a colleague's car and returned to find a smashed window and an empty space under the seat. This happened in broad daylight on a busy road in the middle of the city. Unfortunately, my mom's, my sister's and my passports were in his briefcase, so we had to go through the arduous process of re-applying for visas.

Having a visa in Saudi becomes your identity and the deciding factor at the border. If you do not have a business visa, you may not enter the country. If you do not have a visa to visit your *direct* family members (mother, father, sister, brother, daughter, son), you may not enter the country (although this has changed since we left). All I wanted was for my best friend to come to visit, for my cousins to come and see what our new life was like, but the Kingdom forbade it. It was these laws that made leaving a few years later so hard, as I knew I could never go back.

***

I made one of my best friends, Ashleigh, in Saudi. The country flaunts this unbelievable element of unpredictability, which means you could lose a friend literally overnight. A year and a half after my arrival in Saudi and us solidifying our friendship, Ashleigh left in late 2008. She then came back for a visit as her dad remained in the country, and ended up staying until 2010. On her return our friendship intensified, and I couldn't see myself doing anything without her, my appreciation of her having been renewed. The second goodbye is always the worst—you are more in tune with your emotions and the many notes they can play—so finally losing her again to America, a million miles away, felt like I had lost her altogether.

Amy was another very dear friend in whom I confided almost everything, but I lost her as a friend for disappointing reasons. She was my go-to for everything—for instance, she was the first person to comfort me when I had my very first period and I was feeling embarrassed and confused—and I placed an enormous amount of trust in her. We managed to get ourselves tangled up with the same guy, which became the deciding factor in ending our friendship. I think we have now forgiven each other, albeit indirectly, as all the passing years, and time, have allowed us to heal. Despite all the effort I put into trying to mend the cracks and create something whole again, she lost interest in me. I was younger than her, so she had other friends in whom she could invest her time, who she perceived as more mature and dependable. After a while I had to put myself first to avoid looking like a fool, because I wasn't going to fight any longer for someone who would not fight back. It was upsetting and painful because I thought I had my person to share everything with, where there were no boundaries and honesty was what defined us. But she let me down and threw everything away, like it meant nothing.

She was made aware of a rumour. Whoever told her said I was to blame, knowing the fragile state of our friendship, but she didn't wish to believe me, no matter how hard I tried to get her in my corner. Her defiance and unrelenting belief that I had said those things about her—something I would never have dreamed of doing—drew a line in the sand for me. As a sad consequence, I learned to know myself better and remain true to that, even if it meant no longer fighting for someone who meant so much.

When all these people let me down or weren't around, I had Shane. Shane was my parent figure when I didn't feel like talking to my own parents. He was someone I could look up to and I could write (another) book about all the guidance he gave me. I was such a curious little mongrel and I had so many questions: about the people around us, about Islam (I once asked him if he was 'doing Ramadan' like it was an Internet challenge, instead of asking him if he would be fasting like most Muslims would be), about boys. He was my number one source of comfort, advice, information and laughter, whenever I needed it. He was five years older than me, and the father figure for everyone, but especially for me.

I may not say it out loud, but I still feel as if our bond is intact, and I can't quite compare it to any other bond I've had with another person. He taught me so much that I find it hard to put into words the hurt I felt when he left for university—something neither of us could have avoided or prevented. He had to move on and grow up at some point, I guess. I was only thirteen at the time, so I didn't know what to do with my feelings, but I do know that I felt a huge sense of loss. I couldn't wrap my head around the fact that he was going to be so far away in America, studying a degree, interacting with new people in a different environment, all without being able to see me at the end of the day. I usually sprinted out of my house at any given opportunity knowing he would be there, wearing his infamous, mustard yellow 'comfort shorts'.

Our moments together were precious. He knew when to speak the right words at the right time, and I literally thought that he could do no wrong. He called me his snowflake—a small, delicate yet quite complicated being, unique and capable of creating smiles, especially on his face. I could never melt, he said, so nothing of me would ever be destroyed, but the trick was that I needed to stay away from the flame. Shane created this gentle and warming fire in me that made me feel appreciated and recognised for who I was. He noticed things about me that nobody else, even I, did, and he could communicate with me in ways that made the world feel simpler and more understandable. There was nothing romantic about my relationship with Shane, but he was my guardian angel who sheltered my naïve and innocent self from the bad.

As both of us grew older and started to move on, our friendship became strained. I think he felt the age gap closing. I was an early adolescent, he was in his last year of school, and he started hanging out with different people closer to his age. I no longer saw as much of him, but I guess we were both changing. No one is to blame for this because life was just passing by organically and sending us in different directions, but being the person I was, I wanted to try and fix it. Time went on and the void in me got bigger as I began to realise that I could not do much more to close this hole or mend the cracks. I could only accept that this was the way things were going to be.

Shane came back to visit a year or so later after being in the States and, in his eyes, I was a totally different person. I was no longer his Little Snowflake. Because I still looked at him in the same way as thirteen-year-old Gabi did, I initially felt disappointed in myself for not still being the person he once adored. But I had grown up and so had he. What else could I do? Our friendship struggled to resume its old patterns. I remember playing soccer on the field at Eid during his visit. I felt distracted by his presence on the field, and he said to me, "What has happened to you? Why are you so grown up? You're so different."

I can't accurately describe what this did to me. I was so wounded; my heart crumbled right there on the field. I think what hurt the most was the painful truth of his words. I yearned to be his Baby Snow again but, in that moment, I felt like I had melted.

***

In general, Eid was my favourite place to be. It was like my happy bubble of memories that always protected me from the outside world. During my last week there, in early December 2010, one of the security guards—a tall Pakistani man with a thick moustache—caught up with me when I was walking to the shop. He pointed out that he remembered me from when I was "just a little girl and new to Eid". This tugged at my heartstrings and made me realise that my Eid family was a lot bigger than I had initially thought. Someone like a security guard had noticed and remembered me. I also had quite a special bond with one of the maintenance guards who doubled as a watchman when we played on the soccer field, ensuring we didn't misbehave too badly. He taught me how to play volleyball, drawing on his skills as a young boy playing in the dust in India. I attributed part of my growth as a member of the school volleyball team more to him than my own coach.

The world works in funny ways, making sure you remember the important moments in your life, even if you weren't able to gauge their significance at the time. After leaving Riyadh, I had vivid dreams of Eid that took me full days to recover from, because that feeling of hurt, mixed with nostalgia, can be overwhelming.

What escalated it from overwhelming to painful nostalgia when the dreams first started was the knowledge that I would never live there again.

***

Our three pets joined us in Saudi: a Maine Coon cat very originally named Tom, a Staffordshire Terrier named Stitch, and a Golden Labrador Retriever called Satchmo (after Louis Armstrong). We would not have gone to Saudi, or anywhere else for that matter, if we couldn't have taken our animals with. My dad paid a hefty sum of money to ensure they came directly to us from the airport instead of being put in quarantine. Unfortunately, the compound environment was extremely unsuitable for our dogs, but we made the necessary changes to accommodate them: we dug up our concrete back yard and laid down grass, and my mom walked the dogs twice a day. There are certain things that people simply can't manage without, and have to have at all costs, even when undergoing painful changes in their lives. Our animals were just that. Without our four-legged, panting companions, our family would be incomplete, leading us to the conclusion that home was wherever our animals were. Our Staffie, Stitch, soon became the compound's favourite dog, and people spent a lot of time outside our house playing with her. She had this weird puppy power to convert people who didn't like dogs into people who did.

Satchmo (or Satch) was the grandpa amongst them. He was ten years old when we arrived in Saudi and the most docile, divine dog, who always comforted us when life seemed hard. In the way that things happen with large, ageing dogs, his life became more complicated with the introduction of a multitude of health problems. He lost most of his hearing, and his sight was slowly deteriorating as a consequence of developing diabetes. The diabetes got worse and started to take over his life as he grew increasingly dependent on the insulin injections my dad gave him every morning. This dreadful disease continued to house itself in our dear dog's body, and we could see his chances of ever getting better growing slimmer.

My parents had made good friends with a vet, also from South Africa, so he was often at our house examining Satch. One otherwise normal day he came to check Satch's blood sugar levels and we later found out that this would be the penultimate visit. The next would be to put our beloved dog's life to a peaceful end. I was in tremendous denial about it—Satch had been one of my best friends since I could barely walk, and I really didn't want him to leave us yet. But that was the only way he wouldn't be in pain any more.

I clearly remember saying goodbye to my friends on a Thursday evening to spend the rest of my night with Satch, because it would be our last one together.

He struggled to stand up when he was lying in the kitchen, so I asked my friend to help me push him along the tiled floor to the living room. I spent the rest of the night lying with him on the cold floor, loving him with all I had, clutching onto his fur as I wept into it. I wonder if he knew.

Stitch was such a special little dog, with a personality typical of Staffies. She had so much love to give and was an inimitable element in our world. I had a few younger friends who had a fear of dogs that they couldn't really explain, but spending time with Stitch made that fear disappear.

And then, within the space of three months, the world we had once known shattered into a thousand pieces. We arrived back from a long holiday in South Africa, expecting to come home to an overexcited, frantically panting brown dog, but instead an unenergetic and inexplicably sad little Staffie greeted us. We had never seen her this way before, so we knew almost instantly that something was wrong. We thought she was just hot and dehydrated from the unbearable Middle Eastern temperatures, but there was air-conditioning in every room (a prerequisite) and this mood of hers continued for another month. We called on our vet friend who noticed her abnormally bloated stomach. He suggested she have an X-ray at what turned out to be a very average veterinary practice near the centre of town. We learned through this process that South Africans take animal loving to an advanced level,

45

and so have suitable systems in place for curing their pets. Saudi was quite the opposite, with a lack of resources dedicated to animals and a corresponding lack of love for them.

The X-ray results broke our hearts. Stitch had a tumour the size of two fists dominating the majority of her internal organs. The vet prescribed medication to try to reduce the size of the tumour or prevent it from spreading. She got better for a while, but this didn't last long; it was as if she was trying hard to get well so we wouldn't look so sad all the time. We took her back home and had more X-rays done, but it became clear that the medication was a waste of time and having no effect. The vet informed us that they would have to operate on her to try to remove the tumour, which had now spread to her stomach. They opened her up, and within a few minutes knew there was nothing they could do. The damage was too intense, and the tumour had completely ruined Stitch's insides. My dad came to our school and my sister and I were called to reception, where he just burst into tears. He didn't need to say much more.

My reaction was uncontrollable. I was again in denial that a huge part of my life had been taken away. You never really click in these moments and comprehend that it is all real, that it isn't some kind of twisted dream. But time went on and the reality remained the same. Why *our* Staffie? And why did she have to go in such a gruesome, unfair way? And why were we not warned? She was our permanent bundle of joy, and life all of a sudden felt so much darker.

I went back to the lunch table and told my friends what had happened. I think they were all as distraught as I was. I couldn't control my tears and obviously this drew some attention—a 'friend' let out a small snigger when I told her my favourite dog had passed away. I can't stand people like her who have no decent understanding of my, and my family's, appreciation and adoration for animals. Losing an animal is like losing a best friend.

Only ignorant or indifferent people would say, "But it's just a dog."

Stitch was evidently so much more than that. People on the compound were all silent when they heard the news, and most of them shared my pain, either because they cared for Stitch or they cared for me, and my relationship with her. But, undoubtedly, they loved her in a similar manner.

Hope you're having fun up there, Stitchy.

CHAPTER TWO
School

The school I went to was one of three available options: the American International School of Riyadh (AISR), the Multinational School, and the British International School of Riyadh (BISR). On paper, AISR sounded the most appealing but the educational system was, well, American, and totally different to what we were used to. So, we went with BISR. My sister and I completed the entrance exams and were accepted.

Being new was positively one of the worst experiences I have ever had. And I was new to being new. Because of this, I battled with (what felt like) hundreds of fresh pairs of eyes on me, all at once. Whether they were twelve-years-old or not didn't matter; I felt as if I was going through a screening in each of their minds about what kind of person I was. And look, new girl obviously doesn't have the correct uniform (the shop was out of stock), so even more reason to stare at her. People stared, and talked about me, and asked me mundane questions.

Pleeeeease can this only last a day?

Being in this new school—this new environment with its strange inhabitants—was going to take some heavy adjusting. It was almost the polar opposite of what I had been accustomed to previously. Crawford Lonehill in Johannesburg all of a sudden appeared very comfortable.

Cue flooding feelings of negativity because my parents made me leave my happy place.

Being new made me realise, again, how much I despised change. I hated when it happened, and I hated even more being told: "You will adjust." I refused to believe this. And because of this refusal and my stubbornness, things got a little hard. But I chose the tougher route then, and I still, to this day, do not enjoy change. It makes me uneasy and anxious.

There was a colourful cultural pot of people at this school that I couldn't imagine myself encountering had I stayed in Johannesburg, but I guess there was a reason it was categorised as an 'international' school. There were people from England, Pakistan, Ireland, Australia, and a young South African who had just been thrown into the mix. It was bizarre. I stuck out like a sore thumb, and I wasn't sure I liked it. I met a Dutch girl—an assigned 'buddy' to the newcomer—who helped me find my way around the school. We had discussions about similar Dutch and Afrikaans words, and it was nice to have someone who I had something in common with. This small factor helped me keep things together and maybe forced me to feel an ounce of optimism that things were actually going to be all right.

Even though I was twelve and puberty was still a few miles away, it appeared I was 'fresh meat' and the boys seemed more curious than I was used to because there was a new girl walking around. Looking back, I don't understand this because my scalp was covered with frizz, I had braces, dark leg hair because I stole my mom's razor once and knew nothing about the nature of regrowth, and eyebrows that had separation issues. I managed, however, to meet some stellar boys who all played huge roles in my teenage and adult life, and who remained very close friends throughout my time in Saudi. I belonged to a friendship group of a mixed bunch of people, but they were mainly from the UK; up until the end of year eight there were eight to ten of us, but by year nine, only two of us remained.

People were leaving all the time and I think, despite all the mention of change and struggling to adapt, this is what I found the hardest to accept. People dispersed almost overnight, proving the unpredictable nature of this sandpit. And it sucked. People seemed to trickle through the Saudi sieve-like grains of sand going to another place. The larger stones—us —were left behind.

Time marched on and I arrived at year nine of my academics. It was a confusing year of self-discovery, puberty, more change, bravery, and also a heap of heartbreak and pain. I like to think of this year as the one where I 'blossomed' because I felt like I had grown up a little. I started attracting more attention, I no longer had braces, I felt a little taller and—oh, look—I have boobs now. Because of this and a similar brand of hormones rushing through the bodies of the boys in my grade, I was being noticed more than I was previously. I was constantly harassed by having my skirt lifted up several times a day, boys started sitting with me more often at lunch and attempted to flirt with me. The majority of these boys came from Arabic or Middle Eastern backgrounds. This experience with adolescent boys seemed to me to represent a microcosm of a divisive global society, where the meaning of 'respect' appeared subjective and differed according to the culture one came from. Especially when it came to women.

Year nine was a testing and puzzling time for me. I couldn't make up my mind about what I wanted, who I wanted to be, what I wanted to do with my life. I was fourteen at this point.

Surely, I am strong enough now?

I let people, specifically boys, walk all over me, and my confidence and self-esteem became collateral damage, but I simply did not have the strength to prevent it from happening. If I did, I didn't know how to use it. Outsiders may say that I walked myself into that mess—how boys viewed me and treated me subsequently—because I led them on and made them believe I was okay with what they were doing when I laughed along with them, all because I loved the attention. I was a flirt and it got me into nothing but

51

trouble, because I figured that, to them, I was just something to look at, that the harassment was meaningless.

I went through a phase where I hung out with the wrong people, trying to mould myself to fit in with them, but this cost me dearly. I ended up losing the people who I cared for the most and who valued my friendship, in comparison to the people I was trying so hard to please. Only after three of my closest friends told me I had changed and that I was no longer the person they first thought they knew, was I motivated to do something about this 'new life' I had made for myself. I mustered up a teeny bit of courage where I called people out on their behaviour and learned how to say 'no'—ultimately realising what I was worth and how I deserved to be treated—and boys started backing off a bit (because they weren't getting what they wanted any more), and I made the necessary amends with my best friends. I am so glad they told me what a moron I was being, and I am grateful they made me aware of how I was behaving and the subsequent effect this had on the people I cared for the most.

School was a fun time. I didn't feel too bitter or sullen about going every day. I wasn't a bad student and my grades were where they should have been. I had my best friend, Angie, who was my ninja in crime, to help me through everything, and teachers very quickly got the gist of our inseparable friendship. I envied her because she came across as so confident and was herself all the time, never apologising for it. Not to mention the fact that she was so damn smart, which was intimidating at times. She never left my side, even when she had perfect opportunities to walk away.

My favourite subjects were history and English. History, because we had an awesome teacher with a strong Cockney accent who was incredibly entertaining and did not shy away from tearing homework to pieces in front of the whole class if it did not meet his standards. He always pushed us to be better. In year ten we had a different teacher—his friend, an Irish guy, who was just as entertaining and extremely intelligent. And English, because the teacher we had was as loopy as anything, but they say the best ones always are. She saw how determined I was to be as good as the students at the top of the class, so she always put in as much effort with me. She helped me grow a lot in this subject and as a writer and I never dreamed that her persistent commitment to helping me be better myself would benefit me later in life.

As time went on, school was no longer fun and games. GCSEs started, free time disappeared, parents got stricter, and schoolwork got tougher. My love for the arts and language continued. I chose Spanish, art and history as my electives, with English a welcomed compulsory subject, and business studies and double science as average filler subjects. Art, surprisingly, quickly became my favourite subject purely because of my teacher. Mr Boddington and I developed something akin to a friendship, making my end-of-the-day art classes similar to therapy to me: an escape from the nonsense of boys and the petty dramas that occurred throughout the day. It was, then, an incredibly pleasant surprise to hear from my old art teacher six years after we had last seen each other (in 2016), letting me know that I occurred to him in a dream—even my name—since his move to the island of Rhodes in Greece. I think he was just as taken aback as I was, considering it was Rhodes University in South Africa where I ended up studying for my tertiary education. It's funny, isn't it, how the people from your past never really leave you?

We students shared a sincere dislike for our form room teacher, a lady from India, who proved to be very easy to mock since we were childish teenagers and she made it hard for us to take her seriously. Typical accents from her region of India meant that most of her Vs were replaced with Ws, a fact that caused us to burst into laughter. For example, when explaining the school dress code, she informed us that we were allowed to wear "sleeveless wests under our school shirts", instead of vests. She was our form teacher for our whole GCSE course, which lasted two years, and seemed to have taken an intense dislike towards my trio of close friends. Whenever the whole class wasn't cooperating with her (which was often), including us, she would shout at our trio the most. I had never been sent out of class before in my whole life—because I naturally got along with most teachers—until we were under her 'leadership'.

You may be feeling sorry for her at this point because there's always one teacher who is tortured by her students, but when she commented in my school report, 'Gabriella has brilliant marks in design and technology', I lost any respect I had for her as I didn't actually take D and T as a subject.

I went through a phase in my schooling where my results plummeted. I was failing a few subjects and, because I was a self-righteous teenager, I just simply couldn't understand why. Did my boyfriend at the time, who I absolutely adored, distract me, or had the seriousness of GCSEs not registered in my seemingly sieve-like brain? I desperately wanted to get my act together and concentrate on school, and I tried so hard, but my efforts did not translate into improved grades. Slowly, however, things got better, and we wrote our first external GCSE exam in July 2010, which was double science. I studied like my life depended on it and my marks finally proved that I did, indeed, have it in me to get the grades I deserved. I was ecstatic to hear my results, considering there is very little inclination towards science in any of my family members. My mom got teary, maybe because the little adolescent terrorist that had been living in her house, who argued with her incessantly and convinced her that she 'had this under control and didn't need help', had given her a moment to be proud. The mental block I had towards academics—that I couldn't do it—lightened for a while and my confidence felt like it was on the way to being restored.

In hindsight, studying at an international school in Saudi Arabia was no easy feat. I never acknowledged this at the time because my emotional intelligence did not allow me, then, to see further than my own two feet. BISR did the best they could to offer a schooling experience that was as close to normal as possible to its students. For instance, extra-mural activities, such as sport, are commonly accepted in most conventional schooling systems around the world, but then they don't have sandstorms and fifty-degree weather to contend with. Soccer was my main focus, but I only had to be concerned about it for short, six-week periods each year, because winter was the only season safe enough for us to play outside. Because of the sweltering temperatures in summer, playing sport outside was deemed a health hazard.

Sport at the school was divided into middle school and junior varsity teams, and our soccer teams at both levels were incredibly strong. We competed in a tournament called the International Schools Sports League of Riyadh (ISSL-R) where we were considered one of the teams to beat. The last match I played with my team saw us into the final against the French school. Unfortunately, my teammate swore under her breath and was caught by the referee, who subsequently gave her a yellow card. Obviously, this was unfair to us because the French girls had been swearing the whole time, but in French, and so this went unnoticed. The yellow card knocked us a bit and we came second, but I still thought it was good enough for me.

Another tournament we competed in was the British Schools Middle East (BSME) Games, which, in previous years, were only offered to younger students. We were very excited that we also had the chance to compete in 2009, and entered two teams per group— volleyball and soccer for the boys, and netball and soccer for us girls. Netball wasn't the most popular sport and we had very little time to prepare, so we came stone last as anticipated. It didn't help that they had me on the team, someone who badmouthed netball all the time and didn't know any of the rules or positions.

The tournament was hosted in Bahrain and getting there was a total nightmare for me. Because I had a South African passport, I couldn't enter the country alone unless I had a visa or was driven over the border with my parents. We didn't have time to get the visa, so I drove there with my mom and dad. It was only a four-hour drive, so it wasn't a problem, and my parents were going to watch my games (something that always made me excited). When we arrived at border control, my mom dug in her bag to check she had all the passports— only to find she had brought my passport and two of my dad's, instead of her own. She burst into tears and began frantically apologising to me. This ultimately meant that my mom had to stay in a smelly little room at customs while my dad dropped me off with a guy who was going to take me to the hotel where we were staying. My dad then turned the Land Cruiser around, fetched my mom and drove back to Riyadh, all in the same day. I felt dreadful for my mom, who had obviously made a careless mistake but was incredibly remorseful. I wasn't angry with her because we all have this idea in our minds that moms are perfect and always in control, but she is also just a human being who sometimes makes mistakes. I was just upset she wasn't going to be there to see us kick ass in the tournament.

The games were, overall, a success, and a whole lot of fun. We came last in netball and second in soccer, which felt incredible considering my faulty start in the country and that we were competing against many other schools in the whole Middle Eastern region. And it was so incredibly, meltingly hot, with the rude addition of extreme humidity. Our boys came first in both volleyball and soccer, which gave our BISR sports teams a mighty fine reputation. It was a weekend of fun, bonding, and even the start of my very first relationship with a boy, who was the first person I fell head-over-heels for. (But more about that later.)

I was captain of the middle school women's soccer team in 2009, the athletics squad in 2009, and captain of the BSME soccer team in 2010. My leadership qualities and love for leading were born during this time. I loved being looked up to, I loved that people could come to me when they needed help, and I loved having this unspoken but extremely integral trust between myself and my teammates who shared the same adoration for sports that I did. Playing sport at BISR was a huge part of what made the experience wholesome and filled me with an important sense of self-accomplishment—something I had struggled to find for a good portion of my time there.

There was a programme called the Duke of Edinburgh Award Scheme, which is an international award for young people. We were introduced to it at the beginning of year ten, and so we started off with the Bronze award—one of three tiers. There were requirements to meet, such as providing a service; activity that required action (like sport); and also doing something that required skill, such as learning an instrument. This was all in the hope that we would emerge from the programme as well-rounded individuals with broadened horizons. In addition to this, we went on three expeditions a year and, because it was Saudi, the only place we could go was the desert.

The first expedition was more of an introduction to the award, where we camped on the AstroTurf overnight and completed various activities such as cooking our own food and setting up our tents. Ashleigh and I shared a tent while our other two guy friends—the other half of our team—slept in another. After the pretend camp, we were bussed to the desert where we slept in huge, carpeted Bedouin tents, with boys and girls separated. The first walk started in the morning—a twelve-kilometre trek through barren, rocky desert.

The desert was not romantic or untouched in any sense, as there were broken bottles every few metres with the odd biscuit wrapper littered in between, so the scenery was not enjoyable in the conventional sense. It was deceptively cold that morning, but later turned out to be just another hot day in the desert. We prepared our second meal—breakfast—which consisted of tinned tomato soup on a portable gas cooker. Being so far from a breakfast buffet we would have eaten anything. I had never been so relieved to be home after that weekend, where I could eat proper food, have a shower, and poop in a toilet that wasn't directly on the ground.

The next trip was about a month later and required slightly more endurance than the first. We were left to do quite a lot on our own, like travel twelve kilometres in our group with nothing but a map and our rucksacks—a true test of how well teenagers could adapt to their environment. I remember the first day being a huge struggle, because the air was thick with dust and Ashleigh battled with her asthma. However, we tried our hardest to have some fun, whether our goofiness was a result of heat-induced hilarity or not, but we also had some difficult times where none of us wanted to be together (an understandable consequence of being forced to be with the same people for extended periods). It was like *Survivor* for kids. In a way, though, I can partially thank the Duke of Edinburgh for bringing us, as a friendship group, closer, and strengthening our ties with each other.

There was a third trip, but I am struggling to remember the details. All I remember was sitting with my good friend, Sean, watching the sunset. And there was an idiot who decided to start a rock war, and inflicted injury on a poor, lanky student from our year. Unfortunately, after all of that, I never got my award because I forgot to have my logbook signed by my supervisor.

***

I had never, in my life, had enemies. I loved everyone, most people loved me, I avoided confrontation and conflict at all times, and I had never had any serious fallouts with the people in my life. This, however, changed after my first few years at BISR. I don't think the place was to blame because there was no intrinsic culture of bullying at the school (according to what I knew at the time). I think it was just the period of our lives we were all experiencing, with hormones and teenage frustration to blame more than anything else.

Two key individuals had me convinced that I was not going to make it through my time at school in one piece. There was a new guy from Pakistan named Rudwan, who arrived at the school in 2008. Initially everyone made fun of him because he had more facial hair than any guy experiencing puberty, including most dads, in the entire school. The teasing got to him, so he shaved it all off and ultimately made more friends. I thought he was pretty cool—pleasant and a little bit shy—but, unfortunately, I only ever found out what he was truly like over MSN Messenger. Face-to-face interaction was limited back then as our adolescent selves shied away from any opportunity that was potentially embarrassing, so instant messaging was far safer. It was weird, but our cyber relationship continued and then, one day, he asked me to be his girlfriend over MSN. I said yes, mostly out of flattery because someone liked me—a naïve young girl with braces and very little knowledge of how to make herself look more feminine or attractive. I went to sit with my new boyfriend on the AstroTurf feeling like a nervous wreck, not knowing how to act or behave or talk to this person who was practically a stranger.

I thought you liked him?

I questioned myself, but I was only thirteen, so why did I have such high expectations for myself when I didn't really know how relationships worked? I think we 'dated' for about a month until I came to my senses and decided we should work on a friendship that required us to actually speak in person.

Rudwan later turned into a manipulative, intimidating presence at school that I came to fear. After we broke off our relationship, we became closer as friends, but our feelings for each other returned, feelings that could be justified, and we decided to try dating again. It felt different and I was a lot more comfortable around him at school, and we lasted for a good, few months. I attempted hiding this new guy who had entered my life from my parents, but they found out and totally disapproved of me dating someone from a completely different cultural and religious background. It was the fact that he was Muslim that worried them most, because they had been made aware of how Muslim men in this country treated women, and they assumed he was just like them. I later discovered that the role models in the lives of young Muslim boys teach this kind of behaviour, and they are obviously not born with these chauvinistic views. I tried very hard to convince my mom and dad that he was different, but their resistance continued. But being fourteen, and sure that I knew what I was doing, I ignored my parents and disregarded their thoughts on this newfound relationship.

Rudwan and I broke up again, but I now had real-life experience to draw from to justify my decision. He was incredibly manipulative and shattered any sense of confidence I had in myself. He made me feel small, like a little girl that should feel privileged to be dating him, and often put pressure on me because I didn't want to make out with him when I hadn't even had my first kiss yet. He wanted to have a sense of power over me. He constantly made fun of me for being so 'innocent' and I somehow decided that I deserved better. I made it clear to him that this was the last time we were going to be involved in anything romantic, and he jumped to conclusions, thinking I had broken up with him because

I had started spending more time with another guy friend. We kept our distance and attempted to get on with our normal lives, without each other.

Although I tried to keep to myself and spend more time with friends and family instead of focusing my mind on who I should be in a relationship with next, my progress was hindered by Rudwan's incessant commitment to making my life a misery. He would take any opportunity to hurl some kind of abuse at me, and I struggled very hard to not be affected by this person I had once felt quite deeply for. But I had a fantastic group of friends at the time, and I eventually did move on to someone else. This combination helped me ignore whatever Rudwan had to say to bring me down. However, after the summer holidays in 2009, my world as I knew it was flipped on its head, and I was changed forever.

I had a few friends over to visit me before we had to go back to school for another year of gruesome academics, and we decided to go swimming at the wave pool because we were still in the unbearable throngs of summer. I left my room to change into my bikini and came back to find two of my friends on my laptop, sniggering away at something on the screen. I went over to find out what was so funny and realised I had left my MSN conversation open with another friend, Akeem. My friends were joking away, sending my friend inappropriate messages that were very obviously not from me, but I didn't think anything of it because teenagers will be teenagers, right? I knew nothing would happen because the friend on the other side of the messages knew I wasn't the type to send suggestive messages of that nature to him—Akeem had known me since my first day at BISR—but I was wrong.

The next day, I went to Nick's house—the boy I ended up dating—at Salwa compound and got in the driver's car to go home, extremely happy and full of beans because I had finally had my first kiss with the guy I really liked—and then I checked my phone. I had been tagged in a 'note' (when these still existed) on Facebook titled:

'This is what happens when a South African turns into a whore. From Rudwan, Akeem, and Nader', (a co-conspirator I considered a friend). I knew it was about me, and I knew my ex was the leader of whatever they were trying to achieve by making this note public. He had tagged around thirty-five of my friends and people I knew in the note.

The conversation between my friends at my house and Akeem over MSN had been pasted on Facebook with the caption: 'Hey guys, just wanted you to see what kind of person Gabi really is. I look forward to seeing your comments.' One girl, who was more of an acquaintance than a friend, commented and told Rudwan that it was obviously nonsense and that I hadn't written any of the conversation, and told him to take it off. He tried to defend himself, but eventually he took the note down for her. After seeing this, something inside me felt like it was physically rupturing. Aside from breaking up with him months before, *What had I done to deserve this?*

He brought my home into it by mentioning my nationality and degraded me by creating a false reputation of someone who has multiple sexual partners, when I had only just had my first kiss. My heart shattered. The high I was experiencing from kissing Nick was brutally destroyed and it's a shame that I remember this day as a day where both the best and worst things happened to me at the same time.

The days following this were painful, and I only ever came out of my room to eat. My parents noticed something was wrong and asked if everything was okay. I told them I had been completely and irrationally victimised, for something I didn't do, on a public forum.

I told them the story, saying, "I think I've been made a victim of cyber bullying," and broke down in tears that rolled down my cheeks and onto the kitchen tablecloth.

My dad was infuriated, and shouted, "If we were in any other civilised country, I would sue!" My parents wanted this kid to be dealt with in the most severe manner possible. My dad said he was going to bring up the incident with the school whether I liked it or not, and asked me to give him all evidence of this confrontation. I gave him everything—a copy of the note, the MSN conversation, and a list of all parties involved—which he took to the principal and the head of studies. The principal and head of studies were both new, since BISR had recently changed management, and both were incredibly shocked about what had occurred. They had a point to prove and explained that this kind of behaviour would not be tolerated under their leadership, so they ensured the situation would be treated with the utmost seriousness. It was a week before the school year was due to start, so it was still holidays, but I knew what was coming when the term started and everyone got back. Most people were happy to be reunited with their friends after a long, two-month break, the quad area aflutter with excited chatter about their holidays. I, on the other hand, walked into school terrified and still in a lot of pain.

My peers worshipped Rudwan as he was at the top of what I liked to call the year ten hierarchy. As soon as the news became public, I was constantly bullied for being a snitch and for disclosing to the school what had transpired. If I hadn't allowed my dad to tell the school what had happened, what was I supposed to have done to let Rudwan know that what he did was wrong and hurtful, and that you don't treat people like that? That I didn't deserve this. My dwindling confidence would not grant me the strength to deal with the situation on my own. Confrontation made me nauseous and shaky, and I couldn't look Rudwan in the eyes. He made me feel insignificant, like nothing more than the specks of dust that polluted the Riyadh air. I didn't want to know what would happen if I tried to stand up to him and make him take me seriously: I immediately envisioned my cowering self as he spat his angry words at me. The incident then, apparently, became everyone else's business, while I just wanted to bury my head in the sand. All I needed was for him to be held accountable—which he was—but ironically, I was the only one who continued to suffer. At the risk of sounding like an overly protective mom, I am curious to know what his parents thought of their son at this point. I lost so many people who I considered my friends, until it was eventually just Ashleigh and me sitting alone together at lunch. It was a horribly scary and lonely time.

Rudwan, as well as Akeem and Nader and the friends who had sent the MSN messages, were forced to write a letter of apology. What my friends did was immature and inappropriate, but they didn't want me to get hurt the way I did. How could they have anticipated the nasty turn the situation would take?

However, while I lost a lot of friends I thought cared for me, there was one girl who I wasn't going to miss. Harriet was one of the friends sending rude messages to Akeem on my MSN account, and I realised afterwards that she was a bad influence and not someone I should be relying on. I later discovered that she spoke frequently about me behind my back, and then teamed up with Rudwan in berating me for my supposed cowardly behaviour. My name appeared on their slanderous MSN statuses every day; apparently, they had nothing better to talk about at school, either.

I received messages from people that didn't even go to my school but were friends with Rudwan. One guy was someone I had also been friends with, but who had chosen not to take my side. He and I had a mostly cyber relationship, too, but it was a good one and I loved talking to him. There had even been a short period where we really liked each other (we even saw each other in person from time to time) and bonded over our mutual love for alternative rock music. After the incident, he reminded me that while Harriet—she was a mutual friend of both of us—was at my house earlier this year and we were talking to him over MSN, I had flashed him my bra-covered boobs over webcam for a few seconds, for fun, and that Rudwan's nickname of 'whore' was actually not far from the truth. I have never regretted those few seconds more in my life. It was a mistake and I now know I should not have done it, but I could not predict that the people I had emotional ties with would hold this against me later on.

I needed a break from everyone and to be alone with my headspace, which was rather troubled at the time. So, I ended things with Nick, who I was dating at the time, until I had pulled myself together. I couldn't think straight and I didn't know what to do with myself. I felt like I was the only person in a really dark, cold, sterile room, vulnerable and afraid. I didn't go on any form of social media for about two months, and I didn't discuss what was happening with anyone but Ashleigh, Angie, and my parents. They were the only ones to reassure me that it was okay to go into the school, otherwise I wouldn't have gone at all. I didn't want to show my face anywhere. Ashleigh helped me and comforted me to such a phenomenal extent that, for a short while, I felt like everything was going to be okay.

My social life was basically non-existent for a while, and my group of friends had almost halved in size. I guess it is in situations like these where your real friends shine through and prove the authenticity of the friendship you share. Three months later, Rudwan approached me at school and apologised for what he had done. It was a bit more believable than the apology letter he had evidently been forced to write. Despite the difficulties over these last three years, it was still in my nature to forgive people quickly. That had not changed. I forgave Rudwan, hoping that both he and I would find some kind of inner peace that would help us move on. We had a semblance of a friendship afterwards, but then we fell out again and didn't have anything to do with each other right up until when he left the country for good. I figured out that he apologised to me because all the people who he thought were his friends had left him, too, and were now also making fun of him and pushing him away. The tables had turned. I think he believed that fixing things with me would make him feel better about himself and less alone.

In 2011, when we had both left Saudi, he tried to apologise again over MSN. I was surprised that he thought I would, firstly, give him a minute of my time, and secondly, accept an apology that took him about ten seconds to write on a keyboard, from behind a screen without having to look into my eyes. I was never going to see him again, I absolutely hated him, and walkover-Gabi was in the past. I could never forgive him for everything that he did. It was so gruesome and drained so much life from me and set up a myriad of triggers that would affect me later on in life. One day on our school bus, someone jokingly called me a 'whore' about six months after all the drama (although I still fail to see how this could be used jokingly), and I burst into tears in front of dozens of people. People don't realise the power words can hold.

The second person who inserted a massive speed bump into my life was Harriet—the same Harriet who was involved in the Rudwan drama. She came to the school in 2009 and into my class. I don't remember how we developed a friendship, as she generally hung out with people I didn't have much in common with. But we became really good friends and I found myself confiding in her often, and we usually had a lot of fun together. The more time I spent with her, the more my other close friends told me that I'd changed. I should have listened to them, and I was irritated with myself for being so weak that I was subconsciously changing who I was in order to feel accepted by others.

After the incident with Rudwan, Harriet seemed to distance herself from me, despite her reassurances that things would get better and that our friendship wouldn't be affected, probably because she had also joined the groups of people who stayed away from me for being a snitch. I think she thought I had got her into trouble as she was also told to write an apology letter following the MSN incident with Rudwan. She and Rudwan would post statuses about me online and so it became obvious that, even though the worst part was over, she wasn't going to stick around as my friend. I decided to simply move on and not allow myself to feel too much about it, and I didn't need her friendship.

The real feud between Harriet and I happened in 2010. A new South African girl, Jess, had arrived with her family, and lived four houses down the road from me. Because they had only come in the second half of the year, Jess had been placed in the year below me despite being the same age. She had befriended another girl who was in the same boat as her, who was good friends with Harriet at the time. I was invited to a friend's birthday party at the Diplomatic Quarter, and I didn't want to go because Harriet was going to be there, and because this particular group of people were into drugs and alcohol, which I wasn't (mainly the drugs part).

Jess's dad worked with mine, and so my mom and hers had become friendly. Jess's mother phoned my mom one day asking for advice. Jess had been invited to the same party I had—not knowing that I was invited—and her mother wanted to know if she should let her go. I gave my honest opinion about why she shouldn't go: because Harriet was a bad influence and I didn't want her influencing Jess when she had just arrived in the country. I offered to go with Jess to prevent anything from going wrong. My mom passed on my opinion as well as a rough summary of Harriet's background. But instead, Jess went to another party at another girl's house, and it turned out that Harriet and her friends ended up going there, too. As the night went on, Jess had some drinks and blurted out to Harriet, "You know, my mom told me not to go to the party at the DQ because Gabi's mom said you're a bad influence and that your family is dysfunctional."

You can guess what happened after this. It all came back to bite me. Harriet picked a nasty fight with me over BBM (Blackberry Messenger), saying that my mom was a liar and that I should just mind my own business. She was probably right, but what I had said was told to my mother behind closed doors in the hope that I was preventing someone else from being led astray—and that Jess would not be sucked into the same hole that I was when Harriet and I were friends. However, the argument got progressively worse and the language became more abusive, and some really hurtful things were said about my mom and me, including about our mother-daughter relationship. I ended up deleting Harriet off my phone and my mom apologised to me for exposing Harriet and her family to someone she thought she could trust.

The sad thing about it was that all of it was true. Harriet was getting drunk most weekends, had a bad reputation with the boys, and both her parents had very little involvement in her life or in guiding her in the right direction. So, in truth, I partially didn't blame her for the way she was—she was the product of a family that didn't care as much as mine did. Whenever I come across these situations, I simultaneously feel bad for the person but also very thankful for the family I have.

Up until I left in 2010, Harriet's reputation got worse and worse, and more and more people started disliking her. The word 'whore' was being thrown around again, except I was no longer on the receiving end. She became something like the year's punch bag, but I somehow didn't feel any sympathy towards her. She was a bitch to my best friend, Angie, who I stood up for because I was tired of this person treating others like trash. The next thing, threats were directed at me that she and her friends were going to beat me to a pulp when I moved to the UK for boarding school.

I try to avoid remembering my brief closeness with her because she hurt a lot of people close to me, including myself, so she simply became, for me, one of those people that float into your life and float right out. I wanted to feel sorry for her because she didn't have a strong support system to help her, but I just couldn't bring myself to show any pity towards someone who put so much effort into making my life miserable.

It is frightening what these experiences can do to a person. Here I am, years after the fact, remembering these events as if they happened just last week. Rudwan and I didn't speak after I refused his apology. However, I found out that his mother died from cancer a year or so later, so I reached out to him to pass on my condolences, which he really appreciated.

These incidents have become ingrained in my mind and have formed a constant reference point for the years that followed. People judging from the outside never understand why I always give others the benefit of the doubt, especially those that cause premeditated hurt. I have never been the same since these events occurred because they happened at such a crucial point in my life, when I was supposed to be growing and developing as a person, slowly making my way towards adulthood. Little did I know that I wouldn't be walking confidently towards that part of my life. I would be crawling and broken and still a bit shell-shocked after experiencing what felt like being in an emotional warzone. But I made it nonetheless and the pieces came together nicely after a lot of introspection and support from the people around me. It took me a really long time to re-establish any sense of confidence in myself and I developed an anxiety that was crippling and frustrating, but I tried my hardest to take care of myself.

CHAPTER THREE
Ugh, boys

I seemed to be one of those girls who couldn't be alone. I had to have someone who would comfort me, reassure me, and care for me in the romantic sense. I didn't spend enough time working on myself because I always had this need for a boy to be nearby, and now I deeply regret this. But, then again, what teenage girl doesn't fly through boyfriends the same way I did?

I could go on for ages about the boys I encountered when I was a teenager. They were misleading, selfish, confusing—yet at the time I thought they were the solution to any despair I was feeling. I struggled to find solace in myself without a boy to lean on and pay attention to me and tell me all the things I needed to hear. It was like my confidence depended on them. Even now, from my more mature standpoint, the male species is bewildering. However, being with a boy whether in friendship or in love, and any kind of union between a girl and a boy, a man and a woman, is kind of like a Rubik's Cube: endless possibilities, irritations, but infinitely satisfying when you get the combinations right. When you find someone you match with, you have both truly won.

While most adolescent girls will have experienced something similar to me wherever they live, the culture of boys I became familiar with in Saudi stuck with me. I felt like they were different to the boys from other parts of the world, like they were a different breed altogether, and the theory that 'all boys are the same' didn't apply because none of them were really the same. Saudi was a conglomerate of different nationalities, cultures and personalities, so it is difficult to pinpoint exactly the types of people one encountered. I was integrated into a population of boys from Arab, European, African and American backgrounds and cultures, where each one of them was taught to believe different things, including how they should treat women. I don't want to generalise, because some boys take things into their own hands and formulate their own meanings and beliefs and turn out somewhat respectable, but my fifteen-year-old self could only believe that the mistreatment of the girls around me, including myself, was not because they were innately unkind but that it was someone else's fault that they were that way. It was precisely this factor that separated one boy from the next.

The Arab boys—from Palestine, Sudan, Lebanon, Egypt, Pakistan, India and even Saudi, namely those from Islamic backgrounds—were the ones that most commonly stood out as disrespectful. I could not find common ground with them because our values were so extraordinarily different. As time went on and we all got older, we got along as friends. I didn't have the maturity or social awareness to call them out on their misogyny, whether subtle or blatant, so we coexisted in relative harmony. They were not terrible people in the conventional sense, but their views on women seemed cock-eyed and backwards, and I was surrounded by this attitude every single day.

The Arabs and Muslims of my year at school believed they were kings. Their reputation appeared to be their most important asset, and this behaviour existed outside of school, too. They had this expectation of how everyone they met should treat them, and that they were somehow superior. As it happens in most Saudi high schools, there was a group of boys at my school who were a combination of Arab and Muslim, who kicked people out of their paths if they got in the way, and treated others terribly, with very little remorse. They terrorised the 'nerds' and ridiculed the girls they didn't like or who were 'whores' in their eyes.

There was a certain boy, with few or no friends— he was admittedly different to others in our year—who became a victim of this group's scornful words, and developed a severe case of depression. He was apparently borderline suicidal because of how badly he was bullied and ended up leaving the school to go back to England.

What I couldn't stand, but was too weak to stop, was how terrified people were of them, including myself. They walked through the corridors like an angry mob that owned the streets, making you feel sorry if you crossed their path. How did a bunch of fifteen-year-olds manage to consolidate so much power?

***

Marriage in Saudi Arabia is not the way I have known it to be. At the young age of fourteen or fifteen, I did not know a lot about marriage, except for what I had seen in the couples around me, such as my parents and family friends. I knew that these people had met each other, fallen in love, and eventually decided they wanted to spend the rest of their lives with each other, so they got married. That was normal for me. Swap my position with a fourteen or fifteen-year-old *Saudi* girl, and the narrative is entirely different.

The way I saw it, most marriages in Saudi were largely about ownership. The man 'owned' the girl/woman. Traditionally, as soon as the female shows signs of puberty, she is eligible for marriage. The man cannot be just anyone, he must be known by the family and, in most cases, the marriage will be arranged by the father. Not long after, a wedding ceremony will be organised. I had met a few adults—friends of my parents—who had been invited to traditional Saudi weddings and their stories highlight an experience totally foreign to what I know to be a day of joy, a day where two individuals unite to start the rest of their lives together.

These weddings started around ten p.m. and carried on until the early hours of the morning. This time period, I assume, was allocated so that the order of events would not be disturbed by the five prayer times that occur during the day until the sun sets. The weddings were segregated into male and female sections, where women were allowed to dress as they pleased, as opposed to their usual attire of the *abaya**2 during the day. When it was time for the ceremony, the man was allowed to take his male family members to the bride's section of the wedding where they exchanged vows and were pronounced man and wife. The man then returned to his side and the woman remained in hers, where they partied to their hearts content, alcohol-free, of course.

My view on these relationships was only informed by the research undertaken by my dad, the stories I had heard, and my subsequent curiosity as I grew older. What particularly enhanced my knowledge were the *Princess* books by Jean Sasson, in which a Saudi princess decided to share her horrific experiences of being Saudi royalty—horrific only because she was a woman. To read real-life stories of rape, abuse and blatant discrimination is heart breaking, knowing that thousands of Saudi girls and women were defined as useless, purely because of their gender. It was

---

*2 *Abaya*: A full-length, long-sleeved outer garment worn by some Muslim women.

happening all around me, but just behind walls that were higher than my own.

It is no wonder, then, that a label gradually evolved in my mind that I would attach to most Muslim men and boys because of all of the horror stories and foreign customs I came to know about, supposedly practiced in the name of Allah. The label my parents had in their heads was far more established, so their negative reaction to my relationships with Muslim boys felt justified to them.

The further I progressed into adolescence the more it appeared that the Arab and Muslim boys of my school had very little respect for women, especially the girls at my school, such as myself, who came from more Western backgrounds. It was commonplace to hurl insults such as 'slut' and 'whore' at girls. What gradually became apparent to me was the way these boys used cyberspace as their weapon of choice to expose and abuse whichever girl they were targeting (we all know this is often a tactic used by many teenage boys in general and not only Arab boys, but my experiences were predominantly with the latter). Instead of adopting a courageous stance, they reverted to cowardly behaviour, where they felt safer and less challenged by looking at a computer screen rather than into your eyes. (You can imagine the damage to their ego should a girl attempt to resist them in person.) One can see why it was so easy for Rudwan to do what he did—he didn't have to confront anything in person because he wasn't brave enough. It was far easier to simply ignore any feelings of remorse that he may have had.

As I mentioned previously, Nader, one of three boys involved in the Facebook incident, was my friend. We got very close at one point, another fleeting friendship, but he chose his loyalty to the school hierarchy over me as soon as I stopped giving him the attention he craved. He eventually became part of the Arab mob ruling the school. I was in a confusing situation involving him and Akeem, another close mutual friend, and I remember the confrontation as being petty, due to miscommunication.

The wrong message reached Nader, and shortly after that I received a message via Akeem saying: 'You're a whore, your mom's a whore, and so are the rest of the women in your family.'

As soon as Akeem said, "Nader wanted me to send you this," I almost knew what the message was going to say. Nader knew what words to use to hurt me the most, drawing on how the incident with Rudwan had impacted me, and he knew this would guarantee a reaction out of me. I said nothing to him but decided I would confront him at school a few days later, instead of continuing the conversation online.

"You had no right to say any of those things about my family. You have no place in my life any more, and I want absolutely nothing to do with you," I said, hoping I sounded confident and assertive. But I could still feel my lips quivering, while inside I was nauseous and terrified. I could feel him manipulating me without even saying a word. I watched a smirk creep across his face, which made me want to murder him.

"I want nothing to do with you either," he replied, still smiling. I wonder if I had even managed to get my point across because of how terrified I felt I appeared or if he really was that careless and vindictive.

I eventually gave up forgiving people who had left a trail of hurt and anger in my life. I finally concluded that giving them the time of day and letting them take advantage of me would soon become the natural way for people to treat me. This continues to be a tricky aspect of my life as I am still someone who avoids confrontation at all costs, and trembles with fear whenever conflict arrives, like the horrid uncle you never want to see but are forced to visit at one point or another.

Another guy in my year, Pranesh, who was considered a complete and total nerd, somehow became one of my closest friends. We were on the same wavelength when it came to observing the hierarchy of our year. It was very similar to typical high school movies, where I was complicit in creating this order as the 'hot girl' and he was somewhere in there as the 'nerd'. I wasn't a huge fan of the label I had been given, especially when it became the scapegoat whenever he felt opposed to the things I did.

He would often argue, "Oh, you're too popular for me anyway," when we disagreed. In my head I would never have used my 'popularity' to deem myself more important or superior to the next person. I knew the name of every single person in my year, and I never judged anyone based on their significance in the hierarchy.

Pranesh and I got along very well. He was ridiculously smart with a wicked sense of humour, something I always admired and enjoyed in a person, no matter who they were. I appreciated his honesty, too, as he wasn't afraid to speak his mind. However, I thought—because he was so smart—he knew how to navigate his way around my personality like a roadmap. He knew I was too nice, hated arguing and confrontation, and that I was extremely gullible and naïve. He became the dominant partner of the friendship, and extremely manipulative.

Like the others, Pranesh and I largely spoke online, and this is where most of the abuse took place. He blackmailed me at every given opportunity; this became another prime example of how, at the time, I let people in too quickly. And, it seems, as soon as they were in, they completely took over—like my soft soul was their kingdom to rule. Our friendship was another one that started and ended very quickly, doing a lot of damage in what felt like a very short period of time.

I had unknowingly given someone power, because the higher members of the hierarchy deemed Pranesh powerless as soon as he set foot into school. Without him knowing it, he had taken a small part of me and he never gave it back.

Most people would ask, "How could you let someone who was considered so insignificant completely wrap you around his little finger?" And I never have an appropriate answer because, the thing is, I never 'let' people do these things willingly. I was an open book then and I still am, but these people are the ones who leave books like me dog-eared and tatty. I don't have the liberty or strength of picking and choosing how these people treat me when they take me off the bookshelf.

And after all that, I arrived at a point where I had my very first, proper boyfriend that felt as real as it could be at the age of fourteen.

Crazy, huh, how I kept having my heart broken and still had some left to give?

Nick, the same boy mentioned earlier, was the year below me at my school; we met on the school ski trip to Switzerland in 2009. (When there is nothing but sand to keep school kids entertained, send them to a country with slopes of the complete opposite.) As you can imagine, dating someone in the year below me came with tons of scrutiny. My label of 'whore' was ditched and instead I became a 'cougar', despite the mere months between our ages. For once I cared very little for what people thought about me or had to say as my feelings for Nick made me feel oddly resilient against those who weren't part of what we shared. Our time together was incredibly fun and I'm so glad it was my first proper relationship.

Things were on and off for a while as two very young souls were still discovering what it meant to be in a relationship and to have feelings towards another person. At one point he chose another girl over me—a girl who had far more confidence than me in letting him know she had a crush on him—but that ended just as swiftly as it started because he realised it was a mistake. I really, really, *reaaallly* liked him, and I felt certainty, disproportionate to my phase in life, that our relationship was going to go somewhere. We made our feelings 'official' in February 2010 and were a couple for the rest of the school year. Because of my track record my parents were, understandably, unexcited about it, but they eventually grew to accept the way things were. I had a screw the world attitude and didn't care what anyone had to say. I was stupidly smitten and I, quite literally, wanted to spend all my time with him.

Nick was my very first proper kiss. These, you may or may not know, are *never* cute, or romantic, or as passionate as they appear in films. As much as I felt like I was floating on a cloud afterwards, it was quite possibly the most awkward moment of my life. It was all so typically teenaged! He snuck out of his house to come meet me, and there was what felt like a horrendously long silence before he plucked up the courage to kiss me.

My first thought was, *What on earth am I doing, my tongue is touching another person's tongue, there is spit everywhere, this is weird, make it stop*, but I eventually melted into an infinite feeling of weightlessness. From then on, I found it difficult to control whatever was coursing through my veins. You call it teenage hormones and horniness, I called it love.

Nick and I made many, many memories together, including a self-vetted list of places where we wanted to share more kisses. The more we kissed, the closer we got, and eventually we completed the list. It sounds so silly now on reading it, but I didn't care what I was doing as long as I was doing it with him. It was like our version of *Nick and Norah's Infinite Playlist.*

Like in any relationship, we fought, and there seemed to be a gap in our trust in each other. Trust, for me, is the most important foundation of any union between one human being and another. It felt as if things were falling apart towards the end, either because of the impending natural fizzling out of our relationship because he was leaving for boarding school—a reality neither of us wanted to acknowledge—or because I had stupidly sent a flirtatious message to another boy that Nick happened to read, or because we were in denial that, given any other circumstances, we might have had a chance to advance through our various stages in life together. But he left for boarding school in England in August 2010, and it felt like he took a piece of me with him because I wasn't the same person for a long time after that. In hindsight, my world was very small at fourteen, but it felt like he comfortably occupied a huge space in it. Losing him initiated my first very real, raw, boundless heartbreak. Although you may not think I could have possibly known what love was at that stage, he was most certainly the closest I got to it for the very first time.

Nick became the benchmark for all my relationships that came after him. I was so in love with him that I even sent his mother a message to convince her to 'unground' him when he wasn't allowed to come to visit me (which I figure, in hindsight, wasn't the way into her good books). He made me temporarily (because of the initial excitement of having him in my life that I didn't care about anything else) forget about anything traumatising and hurtful that had happened to me leading up to our entrance into life as a couple. There was something magnetic about him and he consumed all my thoughts, so much so that at times I was looking at the world through love-drunk eyes that could see only him and how special he made me feel. I strived to feel cherished like that for a very long time afterwards and very little else came close.

It was about three months after Nick left for boarding school that I ended up with someone else. *Not long at all for a heartbroken teen to get over herself, right?*

I reverted to my past trend of dating Muslim boys as I then entered a relationship with a Palestinian, the previously mentioned Akeem. You may be confused reading this, considering the ways I described Muslim boys previously and the negative experiences involving them, but it certainly didn't turn out the way I thought it would.

I had known Akeem since I started at the British School, and he'd had a crush on me since that very first year (or so I'd been told). It wasn't hard to deny him the chance to find his way into my thoughts and feelings with his cheeky smile and goofy laugh, but I think I actually adored him. We were the most loved couple in the whole of Riyadh, and I felt so safe when I was with him, and for once I wasn't criticised by those around me, bar a few, for whom I chose to date—except by my parents. He wouldn't have dreamed of hurting me and protected me like I was his hidden treasure, and we never had any silly fights. In comparison to previous relationships that were initially founded on friendship, Akeem and I were 'romantic' before we became friends, and this showed as the relationship progressed. I don't know why it didn't faze me at the time because I would have trusted him with my life and I could rely on him to cheer me up, but, as a boyfriend, surely those things were part of the deal? When I took a moment to reflect, he didn't do those things, ever, as a friend.

I really enjoyed our relationship and I have no regrets about it. However, he did end up hurting me after our relationship ended, when I left the country. He had a brief interlude with someone I considered a very close friend, claiming it was a way to get over me, but only ended up disappointing himself and hurting me badly. And, of course, I felt utterly betrayed by my friend. I finally forgave Akeem, and, by later rekindling the remains of our friendship, got closure. This event has not scarred me the way others have. Akeem and I still talk from time to time and, for some reason, we always remember each other fondly.

Again, my parents refused to support our relationship due to the fact that he was Muslim with a background the polar opposite of mine. Granted, they also wanted me to focus more on my academics rather than on a boyfriend who would inevitably distract me, but he and I agreed to work together to make sure we could maintain our relationship as well as concentrate on school. I tried really hard to convince my parents that he was different and not like other Muslim boys, but the discussion always ended in an argument and I never succeeded. So I stopped letting them in on what was happening between us, not that they really asked how things were. For once, though, I understood where they were coming from—maybe growing a little older helped me establish a different kind of maturity—given that Akeem would never tell his parents about his white, South African, agnostic girlfriend. He told me, later, that he did tell his parents after we broke up and, apparently, they didn't have a meltdown. Then I thought he was different after all, and so was his family. We tried to stay together from afar for about two months after I left Saudi, but it was really difficult, and we ended up agreeing that our time was over. I haven't seen him since.

Tim was a very sweet boy who took me as his date to the Valentine's Disco when we were thirteen years old. We had grown to become best friends since year seven and it was in year eight when he made the bold move of asking me to the disco. I often look back and giggle at how we self-conscious, timid, naïve teenagers behaved. Tim bought me a rose that night, we shared a slow dance with an arm's distance between us, but we didn't utter a word to each other the whole night. I remember being so incredibly nervous because, like I said, I didn't know how these things worked.

In year eight, Tim left for boarding school in England—another companion who left to become re-integrated into a comparatively more normal schooling environment. However, he didn't like it and came back to our school at the start of year nine. I loved having him back and woke up every morning giddy with the knowledge that I would be seeing him at school that day. Our friendship grew into something lasting, honest, and thoroughly fulfilling. It was one of my more meaningful friendships during my time in Saudi; we spoke for hours on the phone every day, despite having seen each other at school that same day. He was incredibly protective of me and was my ultimate confidant when life felt difficult. However, as happened with many of my other male friendships, Tim developed feelings for me that seemed to go beyond a teenage crush. From the end of year nine onwards, Tim's behaviour around me became quite obvious, but I just wouldn't admit to myself that he felt this way or that I could feel that way towards him too. But by December of year ten, Tim and I were inseparable, and it became increasingly evident to both our peers and teachers. When my mom went to parent-teacher evenings, nine times out of ten at least one teacher would ask, "So, Mrs Bellairs, what *is* actually going on between Tim and Gabi?" as if this topic of conversation was the whole reason why we were at the meeting.

As I was his best friend, I knew how Tim felt, but never heard it from him even though I had confronted him about it a few times. Deep down I knew he was scared that this kind of admission could jeopardise our friendship. He also knew about my boyfriend, Nick, who was one of his close friends, so I was sure he didn't want to risk that friendship, too. After a while, Tim and I grew apart naturally. He started hanging out with different people, turning down invites to come over more often, and our hour-long phone calls became less and less frequent, until they stopped entirely. It saddened me that two people who had shared such a beautiful friendship could very quickly end up walking past each other in the school corridors without batting an eyelid.

Before our friendship died down, there was a moment in school I will never forget. Tim and I were in the same history class. Our teacher, Mr Banks, was the fun, jesting kind of teacher that you could simultaneously enjoy while still learning a lot. He lived in the same compound as Tim. This meant that Mr Banks often socialised with Tim's parents and was well aware of his crush on me. One day in class, he asked Tim if he had ever invited me out on a date. I was sitting next to Tim and shook my head in bewilderment. Following this, Mr Banks asked, "Tim, what is wrong with you? Ask her out on a date! In fact, do it right now. And get down on one knee."

Tim, with his reputation of being the class clown and having overwhelming confidence, did not hesitate, got down on one knee, took hold of my hand, and asked me if I would go out with him. Obviously, I said yes. This moment stuck with me for a very long time afterwards.

Tim and I both began to change. He started having random hook ups on the weekends and I remember being quite disappointed that I was hearing this news from other people. I still expected my best friend to confide in me like he had in the past. I neglected a lot of people, too, Tim included, and spent a lot of time with Nick during whatever moments I had free. There was a knock-on effect as Tim and Nick grew apart as friends, too. I have a few small regrets attached to this period because I never wanted to be the person who pushed everyone away to be with someone else.

My rational voice, as well as everyone else's around me, told me, "Of course he is drifting away. Look at what you've done to cause it: the boy loves you and you are dating his friend," but I had a habit of suppressing this voice in favour of sticking my head in the sand and pretending it was all everybody else's fault. I still had not had the moment with Tim where he admitted his true feelings, and if I did confront him about it, he denied everything, so that also contributed to my confusion. I reasoned with myself that I couldn't use Tim as an excuse not to pursue the wonderful relationship I had with Nick. My friendship with Tim was truly special and I figured it must have been really hard for him to watch the one he loved being loved by someone else.

Tim eventually admitted his real feelings to me, but only after I had left Saudi. Hearing what he had to say by putting those years of deep feelings for me into words made me realise I was an idiot.

At the time I thought: *You are so dumb. You chose the friend of this magnificent boy, who clearly adores you, and now you cannot go back. You are an idiot.*

I felt terrible because I felt like I hadn't even given him a chance, but at the same time we were like a classic example of poor timing, where the one just misses the other in an overlap that could have led to something akin to magic. Simultaneously, though, there was nothing I regretted about my relationship with Nick, which contained the right kind of magic for me at the time.

If I were reading this story, I would think this part was incredibly anti-climactic, because *they never got together*. Tim and I did end up dating. We both landed up in England at the same time for our final years of school, and he accompanied my family and me on our trip to settling me into my new boarding school. It was then that we decided we were going to be together and not waste any more time, because now he was at least in the same country as me. We gave it a good try. I suspect it came a bit more naturally to him than it did to me because I still viewed him as my best friend, but there was something that felt forced about it. This will be explained in another part of this book.

I have no more stories about boys, I'm afraid. I feel like I needed to tell these anecdotes, interwoven between the other very real experiences during my time in Saudi, because they hold many lessons about what it means to be a young girl in an environment like Saudi. I told myself, when writing this book, that I would tell stories but also impart knowledge that I gained during this rather treacherous, but worthwhile, journey.

All I can advise is, if you are a young girl reading this, treat yourself the way your mom treated you when you first came into the world—like a porcelain doll, delicate and perfect, to be handled with care and love, and only to be made to smile and laugh. You should not be denied the chance to be happy.

CHAPTER FOUR
Family: one of nature's masterpieces

I am limited by words to describe the relationship I have with my family. Moving from our home in South Africa to the most unimaginable place in the world did many things for us—some good and some bad—but most of all it made us stronger.

My dad was the reason we went to Saudi in the first place. It seemed to me, at the time, that the future of my family revolved around my dad and his work. He left his job in Johannesburg for Al Rajhi bank in Riyadh, the biggest retail bank in the Middle East. After a year or two he moved internally to Al Rajhi Capital, their investment bank, which was a lot smaller. The money he would be earning was the magnet that attracted us, not because of bragging rights or to indulge in luxury, but because it would solidify the foundations that would strengthen our ties and allow new opportunities for my sister and me. The zero-tax benefit was a massive influence in our decision-making, too. All the money my dad earned would be going straight into the different facets of his life, unlike the harsh income tax he had experienced in South Africa. Harsh, because there was so much he envisioned for his family and himself and he had to 'give it away' to the South African Revenue Services. It became glaringly obvious that the tax he paid was not going into the further development of our beloved country and this was a frustrating reality to confront.

While this may sound like all that is needed to keep a man happy, it appeared there were many other aspects that could very easily drown out any career-related happiness and fulfilment. My dad's work environment in Riyadh was not conducive to productivity, or solid or trustworthy relationships and high morale. He felt that the Arab community, who were the majority group in the bank, threatened his position almost daily. He knew they had the power to send him across the border if he caught them on a bad day. The relationships he had with them were purely superficial and professional, nothing more and nothing less. While you don't commit to a job to make friends, being in such a sterile environment is enough to make one leave on one's own account. This affected my dad badly. It became apparent that he strongly disliked his work environment, and held it together only by the thought that he could go home at the end of the day to his family. And that this experience was all going to amount to something really, really amazing.

By the time December 2010 came, my dad was ready to leave both the bank and the country. He often remarked that it was an awful, soul-sinking feeling to walk into the building where you worked and to not know whether you would be walking through those doors again the next day. It was terribly unsettling, for all of us, to live with that kind of uncertainty. Over the four years we lived in Saudi I lost count of the number of times that we thought, *We're going to be gone soon.* Then the end of 2010 came, and the decision was made for us. My dad was made redundant and we were told to be out of the country within two months. Because December holidays were coming up, my parents decided we would make our exit then, as it was two weeks away. So, I had two weeks to pack up a life I had just started to love.

***

The words 'blossomed' and the like, are often used to describe the transition from pre-teen to teenager. Change is in the air, your body is changing, and your view on life is changing, too. It's an exciting time because wow, look at you, you are blooming into a young adult and the world is your oyster and there is a wealth of opportunity out there and soon you're going to be having babies.

No, not me.

I did not blossom into adolescence; I was catapulted into it and I landed flat on my face. What an awful, awful time of my life. I hated everything, I hated everyone, and I just wanted to be asleep. All. The. Time.

There was a lot of arguing in my house. I was the leader of my own adolescent terrorist group, with only myself and my heavy metal music bands as members, and I would quite literally scream at whoever placed a toe out of line. For my thirteenth birthday I was given my first laptop—the latest Sony Vaio in a blush pink— and within a week of owning it I managed to have it confiscated by my parents. At the same age, I set up a Bebo account (a baby version of MySpace that all my friends had) behind my mom's back, even when she explicitly told me not to (hello, first grounding). Things were volatile, and I can't remember ever being nice to anyone in my family. (To my family: *Thank you for not putting me up for sale online during this incredibly horrendous time.*)

Thankfully, this kind of behaviour is not unusual (although I wish my parents had let me know at the time) and I realise how troublesome I must've been. Although this happens to many families, it doesn't mean it doesn't take its toll. My relationship with my family felt fragmented and I felt like an outsider, but only because I had placed myself there. Believe it or not, I managed to grow out of this dark phase and re-enter the world as a semi-decent human being who could say nice things and love her family (even her irritating dork of a sister).

My dad and I have a unique father-daughter bond that thrives off our friendship with each other. He is one of my best friends, and that will never change. I can't quite recall what it was like looking through my selfish teenage eyes at the time and saying the most hurtful things to my sister and mom and feeling very little remorse, but what has always remained is that I could not cope with any look of disappointment in my dad's eyes. When he was angry with me, I felt it on a deeper, different level, and I hated it. I can't quite put my finger on exactly *why* it was different to the rest of my family, but it may have been because he and I are so much more alike: confrontation and tension are things we both avoid like the plague.

Our humour is often scarily in-sync, and awareness of our own emotions is something we are able to only identify in one another. I never made my love for my dad obvious when I was younger, but I cannot gather enough words to explain how grateful I am for everything he has done for us. Although he has lived for many more years than I and has a more experienced view on the world, I cannot help but say I am proud of him. Coming from a tiny beach town called Margate on the south coast, in South Africa, he could have ended up where his parents thought he would—as his mother's hairdressing assistant in a deteriorating tourist destination. But he was so much larger than that.

After finishing school at Port Shepstone High, the next move would obviously have been university, but his parents did not think this step in his life was necessary. At eighteen he joined the army (which was still compulsory back then) because this was the only other natural move post-school. He returned with nothing but poor hearing, thanks to exposure to extensive shooting, and excellent ironing skills. He then enrolled at an agricultural college with the hope of becoming a farmer, because this was a prosperous path to follow back in the day. After his stint at this college—when he also met my mom—he took out a loan from the bank to fund a degree in agriculture from the University of Natal (now the University of KwaZulu-Natal), because his parents (a hairdresser and a policeman) could not afford the tuition fees. At that time, he became part of the Standard Bank graduate programme—a programme still held in high esteem—and entered the world of banking. His progression from agricultural banking to investment banking was purely by chance. His offer letter was a reused template for another position, but with his name on it. When he queried this, his superior simply said, "Hmm, that's strange. Well, do you want the position anyway?"

And so began his journey, into the world of investments and corporate life. Thanks to this career move and substantial savings from living in Saudi, my dad was able to fund my last two years of schooling in the United Kingdom at a prestigious school, plus all the years before that, including life in Saudi and many exciting trips abroad.

His financial support was one thing, but his emotional support was another. When I was in the teeth of my angsty adolescence, he was the one adult who could still make me smile (because, obviously, no adult was cool enough to do that if they were lucky enough to even come near me). We didn't get to spend much time together in Saudi because I was out of the doors of my house as quickly as I stepped through them after school, to play soccer or swim in the wave pool, but whenever we were together it was always good. And it continues to be good. My dad's and my relationship was one of trust, transparency and love, and it was all without any effort.

My mom is a passionate photographer. Living in Saudi, with very little opportunity for employment, she had a lot of time to dedicate to her art. Up until the day we left Saudi she had her own little studio in the study room, where she ran her own business called Desertcrew Photography (which is still the business name today). She became incredibly successful, eventually taking photographs for the school as well as photos for weddings and prom dances. Her business was mainly focused on family and child portraiture as it was her favourite and most enjoyable style, and this added fire to the beautiful photographs that came out at the end of each shoot. She displayed most of her photographs in black and white because, to her, the pictures had to speak for themselves.

There was a family in her studio almost every weekend and she started to gain some financial independence—something very rare in our environment—while her photography became another bridge to meeting different people. She also took pictures for the pure love of it, where she captured unseen moments of our trips away: members of the local village in Zambia who had probably never seen a camera before, or of wild vultures coming to feed in barren Namibia. She had the patience, passion and knack for snapping moments that seemed everlasting, and I will always admire her for that. She has passed on a love for capturing these rare moments to me, and our mutual interest in photography is something we have bonded over.

Our relationship was difficult when I was growing up as a teen. It is obvious that tension between a mother and a daughter is likely to brew at some point or another, but this doesn't mean it was ever easy. When I was younger, we were each other's best friend, but as I got older this seemed to change, to morph into a relationship where I was the unmanageable teenager and she the hassled mother running out of solutions to handle her child. I gave my mom hell and she said of me what many mothers have said of their teenage daughters: "You changed almost overnight."

Literally the day I turned thirteen the changes kicked in, and this dark void between my mom and I started to grow, even forcing her to order books online like, *How to Manage Your Satanic Teenage Daughter* (or something very similar). Although I had barely thirteen years of experience on Earth, I traipsed around like I had been poisoned and hard done by, like I *deserved* something. I hated knowing this version of myself but, actually, *did I know myself at all?* I certainly wasn't the Gabriella my parents brought up so lovingly and of whom family friends spoke so fondly.

The moment I gained some hindsight and perspective, I wanted to start backtracking.

How dare I treat my family in this repulsive way, why did I say such nasty things?

I didn't know if I should've blamed the sudden rage of my hormones—the civil war going on in my body— or had I actually *chosen* to go down this tumultuous path? I was not presented with answers. All I know is that everyone in this path I had either willingly or unwittingly followed, had been caused a lot of hurt. I disrespected my parents, bullied my sister, and let myself down. I felt like I had no control.

For instance, when I was in a good mood and thought things were going fine, the rest of my family were the opposite. Of course, in those moments I wanted the storm to calm, but things were out of my control by then and the damage was done—my family was stagnant because of me. I betrayed their trust by setting up a social media account they had strictly forbidden, withheld the information about my Pakistani boyfriend, made little effort with my academics, and was a general nightmare to be around. It finally dawned upon me that I was turning into the rebellious teenager every family is warned about.

There were a few moments in my mom's and my relationship where we were holding each other, tears leaking down our faces, asking ourselves, "Where has our relationship gone?" We saw glimpses of our connection every now and then, but it was fleeting and not enough to force my head into the right direction— the direction where I woke up and realised that without my mom, I'd be a dribbling mess, with no clue how to handle life's hurdles. There is a synergy between us that I never acknowledged when I was young and selfish, which is stupid because she knew me better than I knew myself. She knew when something was wrong, she knew when I was hiding something, and she knew that I had a lot more to put on the table than I was doing back then. I was a surface-level version of myself that chose the easy route whenever it presented itself, no matter what situation I was in.

I have forgiven myself for that period, and I hope my mom has too, because the Gabriella she knew and loved eventually came back in full force. There were a few let downs along my path of self-discovery, but perfection is never something we have strived towards. Our imperfect relationship has blossomed into the only thing I know now to be the most perfect, flawless element of my life. Again, with the benefit of hindsight, our move to this foreign land appeared seamless all because of her.

My sister, Kate, is two and a half years my junior and I was not ready for her when she entered this messy world. By that I mean: *How could I have been expected to live under the same roof as someone who was literally the opposite of me?*

When she was born, I was upset—all attention was now on her and not me. She was a lot quieter than me, and then she grew up to be a giant pain in my ass. But who knew that eventually she and I would grow to know each other better than anyone else? That she would turn into such a wise voice in the world, and that I would love her as my sister, best friend and confidante.

Kate had many, many oddities, both growing up and in the present day. We all think that she spent most of her time being quiet as a child in order to think about all the ways she could be a nonconformist. Unfortunately, this has meant that she has experienced a lot of hurt because people didn't understand her in the way I did, the way that only a sister could understand. Other times, though, it was a source of entertainment. We were once on a plane to Cape Town, our first trip on an aeroplane, and she received a cup of orange juice with her meal. She proceeded to tear open her sachet of salt and pour it into her juice. We all watched, confused and stunned, and saw the concern wash across her face then, too. We asked why on earth she had just poured a sachet of sea salt in her orange juice, and she replied very blankly, "Oh, I thought it was sugar."

This did still not help because I have yet to come across a human being dissatisfied with the artificial sweetness in commercial orange juice. But she was not fazed, and she maintained that her orange juice needed additional sugar.

When we re-watch old home videos, it becomes apparent that I was the peculiar one. My quirks included putting worms in my mouth after it had rained and nagging my dad for the video camera every time I saw it was focused on me, ultimately ruining a short portion of the video that was planned. Kate was the quiet one. She was sick a lot when she was little with ear infections, so maybe she couldn't hear much either. As we grew up, I became more normal and she a little strange. She often had us all in hysterics because she had a natural way of making people laugh, and other times she made us giggle because we simply could not believe the things she would say or do (refer to orange juice incident above).

We had a lot of fun together, especially when we went on holiday. Like every normal sibling relationship, we fought a lot, mostly about petty, ridiculous things: who stole whose hair tie, what we wanted to watch on TV, making sure we didn't have the same hairstyle on a given day. We got over these issues relatively quickly, but there was one pressure that would never go away: my job as a role model to her. Now, as I sit here in my own flat that I pay rent for (well, some of it—starting salaries suck but my subsidising parents are awesome), with my laundry folded and me sipping a glass of wine, I have the experience and perspective to feel confident in my guidance towards her. But back then, when adolescence had me in its grip and she came home from roller blading around the compound to find me reeking of alcohol, I imprinted something in her mind's eye that meant she could no longer look up to me.

She was so young and still figuring out the world, so how on earth could she forget coming home to a drunk, yelling sister who she was, just the other day, playing UNO with? I hope that she grew up to understand, having gone through teenage years herself, that your body and mind don't feel like yours when you have hormones, peer pressure, boys, bad habits and seemingly overbearing parents crashing over you like nasty tidal waves. Since it happened to both her and I, and in two very different ways, I still wish I had put my 'grown up pants' on for her. I wish I hadn't succumbed to the rebellion my previous self had been sucked into—or sometimes been drawn to—and had just been a good big sister. And I wish she could know that I am really sorry I wasn't there for her more but that I'm still really proud of her, as she also overcame a lot in her little life.

My sister has never been the type to speak about her emotions, especially since her interpretations of what happened around her started to develop. I, on the other hand, seemed to be overflowing with this temptation to shout about how I was feeling all the time. These opposites were not complementary. For Kate and me, the moments where we could talk about what was really going on with our sisterhood were fleeting, frequently initiated by me because, even if the issue was of her stealing my socks, I needed closure on our conflict whereas she could move on within a few hours.

Although I learned, at varying paces, from the mistakes I made, I wonder if she learned from them too? She made mistakes as she got older but the tenacity with which she faced life amazed me. At the age of twelve or thirteen she was so confident in herself that I was green with envy. *Why could I not have been so sure of my place in this world that young? So much could have been avoided.*

I love my sister fiercely and, as much as I have been tempted to shelter her from the ugly sides of the world and all the hurt it could bring, I had to let her go—I had to let her venture off into both the brightness and darkness on her own. She has surprised us all and made us think twice about things we adults thought we had figured out already, and tackled things we underestimated her for. She is just another example of the strong women that run through my family and I look forward to taking on the universe with her. What a force we will be.

Kate has an extraordinarily alternative view of the world and the way it works. Because of this, her approach to life is rather unusual. She once told me that she was disgusted that I didn't moisturise my entire body every night because she was convinced this was an integral part of personal hygiene. She also once shouted in dismay when we went to the shopping mall because someone had parked their car in a disabled parking, thinking that the parking space was for the actual wheelchair as indicated on the parking sign. But to say her view is strange is not to say that it is wrong, as she has amazed us many, many times with her wise nuggets of wisdom, purely because she has a remarkable talent for looking at things differently. Her thoughts are often black and white while mine are very much in the grey area, and this has pitted us against each other on more than one occasion. Unfortunately, there was a substantial time in our lives where we battled to see eye-to-eye.

For most of her life Kate was the hard-headed sister with a screw you attitude, and I the sensitive, tender soul. We would struggle to have conversations about what was going on in our lives because she would often have a get over it approach when it came to my issues, not realising that some of the things she said were upsetting. But as our age gap narrowed, she started to understand me a bit more—and I her—and we accommodated our differing personalities. And we both realised that there was a lot we could learn from each other.

She is one of the funniest people I know and is also wildly talented. Even though I was the musical member of the family for a long while, she took us completely by surprise when she gave us a private concert when she was around fourteen, singing Adele's *Turning Tables,* with the most beautiful voice that *we had never heard before.* She took things further and taught herself piano via YouTube and proceeded to produce covers of her favourite songs. She was truly living up to her name as the dark horse in our family, and we were so grateful that she shared her talent with us.

Time went on and we basically started to get to know each other, despite having been sisters for as long as we had both been on the planet. There was a time when I worried that she and I would become those sisters that grew apart and never contacted each other, despite my parents' efforts to unify us. Thank goodness we will never end up this way.

***

Travel was one of the many gifts that living in Saudi gave us. We were almost slap-bang in the centre of the world, meaning we had so many different countries waiting for us to visit them. I fell in love with the strange smells of the London underground, fought my way through week-long fog in Hong Kong, and shamelessly lived like a fourteen-year-old child during a visit to Disneyworld in Florida. I caught swine flu in Mauritius but still consider it one of my favourite holidays, and climbed up mountainous sand dunes during my dad's birthday trip to a desert resort in Abu Dhabi. The excitement of landing in a foreign country never dulled and it meant I had another opportunity to spend time with my family, with different flavoured foods and spectacularly coloured sunsets as our backdrop. Being on these holidays made me realise that I took time with my family for granted. As much as I loved acting carefree with my friends in the compound, the things I thought were hugely important to me seemed to disappear when I spent focused time with my family.

Our last holiday while in Saudi was the trip we made to Abu Dhabi for my dad's birthday. We went to the most stunning resort surrounded by nothing but the burnt-orange dunes of the desert—my favourite kind of oxymoron at the time. In my entire four years of being in Saudi I had never done the dune bashing or camel riding that everyone seems to do in their first few weeks of arriving in the country. On our first day in Abu Dhabi, we climbed aboard a Land Cruiser and headed for the dunes—those towering, intimidating, conglomerates of teeny tiny grains—and drove at ridiculous speeds up and over them. It was so much more authentic than a rollercoaster, and the reward for not getting paranoid was the watercolour-like sunset we got to see at the end. One thing I learned from being in the Middle East was that although the majority of the land is made up of the same sand, no sunset was ever identical. If Mother Nature had been able to put it in slow motion for me, I could have sat for hours watching that burning ball of gas descend beyond the horizon.

Another day of desert-like activities arrived and we went riding on camels into our second Abu Dhabi sunset. Many people found it incredibly unusual that I had never ridden a camel since being in Saudi, as camels were the only animals the Saudis cared about and appreciated. It was a weirdly peaceful experience, and I found camels beguiling creatures; they were cute in an ugly way, kind of like pugs. We weaved through the desert dunes on these huge animals who, despite their size and awkward stature, almost tiptoed on the sand like ballerinas silently fluttering across a stage. We stopped to climb some towering dunes to watch the sun set and let the camels rest. The sun always seemed prettier dipping behind the dunes because it felt like you were the only person watching. *The people seeing you next are lucky*, I thought about the sun, but then I realised that the sun could only be this beautiful here, in this moment.

On our last night in Abu Dhabi, 16th November 2010—and the whole purpose of us being there—was my dad's birthday celebration. My parents' room had a huge balcony and we had organised food to be delivered where we could use the braai (barbeque) to cook dinner. What is still apparent is that no matter where we are, you can't take the braai out of us! We had champagne and ordered shishas (or hubbly-bubbly) for all of us to share. Kate, at the tender age of twelve or thirteen, clearly had too much and woke up with a 'shisha hangover' the next day and could barely move. It was very obviously a special night and I envy my dad for having had a birthday that we still talk about today. We used my dad's iPhone to play music, sang loud and proud to our favourites, and enjoyed each other's company like we were the only human beings left in the world. Even more, we were all intrinsically, unapologetically ourselves. I forgot about the woes that came with daily life in Riyadh like they never existed, and about the reputation I thought I had to fight to uphold, and it felt like I was seeing my family through new, clearer lenses.

This night was so memorable to me for so many reasons. It felt like, leading up to it, there had been a series of warnings that said, 'You know, if you keep acting like you have been, you face the potential consequence of irreparable damage with the only people who will ever see you for who you really are.'

What I could lose was right in front of me, as clear as day. It was also our last holiday as a Saudi Arabian expat family so there was a lot of sentiment lacing our interactions, and nostalgia and fiery love and care for one another. It was the greatest 'full stop' to an often testing, sometimes gruelling, but overwhelmingly exciting period in our lives.

There is no way to conclude this chapter other than by saying that my family are truly my ultimate solution to comfort, trust, and endless love. I count my lucky stars every day that we made it through things that could have had us hanging by threads, to emerge as an unbreakable unit that went on to take on the world with a fire that many only dream of.

CHAPTER FIVE
Friends who told me when my face was dirty

When I left Johannesburg, I was furious to be leaving my best friends behind—the people who I was convinced were my 'ride or die' mini-community set to be by my side for life. I was certain they could never be replaced and that my time in Saudi was just going to be a period in my life where I floated along, did my own thing until it was all over, and could then go back to *my* people who knew me inside out. There was no time or space or energy for anyone else in this new, foreign country of mine.

But I should have been permanently braced for pleasant surprises. I had no idea that, upon leaving Saudi, coming with me were incredible, durable, worthwhile friendships with people who I had welcomed into my life on an everlasting, loving basis. As with many friendships, it did not happen automatically and it was a long and selective process—testing, too, because there were some friends whose light got dimmer in the dark times until their light eventually went out, and others who burst through with brilliance. It was akin to a filtration of something rocky and impure, where the products at the end were the people I could eventually rely on, care for, and be cared for in return in Saudi and for the rest of my life.

Angie was my best friend inside and out of school. Sure, we hit some bumps along the way as we both matured at different rates and our period of self-discovery sometimes led us in opposite directions, but we always came back to each other. Whenever I needed honest advice that went deeper than the surface, or words of comfort that would help calm me down and put things into perspective, I went to her. Our friendship solidified in year nine as she and I were the last ones standing after a bout of family decisions sent other friends in our circle back to their home countries or to different postings, depending on their parents' jobs. Although year nine brought us close together, it was also an incredibly testing period as it was the same year, I became friends with Harriet.

Angie was upfront and did not mince her words; I was changing, and this change correlated with my newfound friendship with Harriet. She (Angie) didn't like the fact that I had drifted so far, both from who I was as a person and from her as my closest friend. At that point in my life there weren't many other people who would do that for me, either because they were too self-absorbed themselves or actually didn't care enough to confront me about the person I was becoming. Angie didn't tell me these things to make me angry or to start a fight—she told me because she had a genuine investment in our friendship and wanted her old friend back. Whenever we had arguments, I would say something funny to her in my attempt to diffuse the tension and she, in turn, would laugh. That marked the end of the disagreement and indirect acknowledgement that things were going to start going back to normal, that I valued what she told me and agreed to do something about my situation. It was both refreshing and reassuring that we simply could not stand arguing with each other and wanted to be in each other's corner all the time.

When my popularity seemingly shot through the roof and more attention was being paid to me since I was no longer the gangly girl with a mono-brow, frizzy hair, and braces, I neglected my friend. Angie saw right through me and knew that superficial acceptance had become important to me, but that I was weak in pushing it away. I, in turn, understood that I was disappointing her. Once my head became clearer and I knew what I wanted—to go back to the beginning with Angie, to our inseparable, happy friendship—I realised how selfish I was to chase something so empty when I had such a wholesome friendship on offer. Thankfully, from year ten onwards, she and I became closer than ever and once again truly the best of friends.

Angie had such a phenomenal sense of humour—a wicked combination of intelligence and pure funny. We shared many hilarious moments. I once had a cramp in my calf and announced this to her, followed shortly by,

"Wait, isn't a calf a baby lamb too?" A random and obviously stupid question to ask that resulted in an uproarious laughter. This was the start of many insider jokes we repeated to ourselves during our times at school. She called a spade a shovel, too, and would not hold back in speaking her mind when she thought something was wrong. This is a fearless and incredibly grownup trait for a fourteen or fifteen-year-old to possess, so sometimes it got a bit much, either because I'd find it unnecessary or because I didn't like to be told I was wrong (another shining quality of being an adolescent). But most times her brutal honesty helped paint a picture for me when things were looking a bit fuzzy, and I admired her for that. Other times her outspokenness was extremely entertaining. The resident bully in the school year often picked fights with her and decided, very bravely, to call her stupid.

She snapped back with, "You're calling me stupid? You probably wrote your maths exam with a crayon."

I hated how so many people picked on her for no reason that was ever good enough. It was mostly the top-of-the-hierarchy Arab boys who wanted to remind her where she stood in the pecking order, but Angie's intelligence and brazenness made her indestructible. She was on their hit list because she was not their idea of what a girl should look like or how a girl should be— she was too different, and they knew it, but they couldn't stand it, mainly because they knew how incredibly smart she was, and that their jabs did not affect her. She had lovely thick, brown hair but didn't wear make-up when other girls were already familiarising themselves with mascara; she had very fair English skin as opposed to tanned, olive skin; she loved English punk rock more than anyone I knew and pronounced 'three' as 'free' because of her accent. She was her own, established person and I was jealous of this, but it was for this reason that other people in our year couldn't handle her. I can only attribute this to an intimidation and threat to their power that they wouldn't admit to.

Angie was there for me from the very beginning and stuck with me through all the bullying drama that infected my self-esteem. She wasn't much for expressing feelings of fondness, but I like to think I was that person to her, too. I at least made sure she knew that should she ever feel like she needed to open up, I would be there for her. There were other people she became close to, but our friendship was special and we both knew it; she is still lodged in my head and heart. I met up with her in the UK after a period of seven months of not seeing each other and it was as if I had seen her just the day before—an example of a pure friendship built on the right things, destined to last. The first and last time I ever saw her cry was when I left Saudi, which meant an enormous amount to me and reaffirmed the seriousness and depth of a friendship I will always cherish.

The next person to join Angie and me in establishing our group of misfits amongst a group of tyrannical teenagers was Andrew. He was the funniest guy I had ever met, with the special knack of causing me to be paralysed by laughter. He would also lend a hand whenever I needed someone. This unique individual was so many people mixed into one body, but was also a frequent victim of scathing words from the top of the hierarchy that criticised his unusual heritage and his approach to life. Andrew was half-Thai and half-English, possibly three heads taller than me, with size-ginormous feet, and I regarded him as my own personal, gentle giant. He was rather chubby, which made him the perfect target for the bullies at school, but he was so resoundingly okay with who he was as a person that he had no problem standing up for himself. Because of his size I am sure he could have knocked out any bully with one, swift motion, but he was such a softie that I don't even think the thought ever crossed his mind.

Andrew was super-special. He and I only became close in year ten, despite him being there in year seven when I arrived at the school and already a member of the group I joined. All I knew, then and now, was that he always made me laugh. Up until I left in year eleven, we started a tradition of epic goodbye hugs where he'd pick me up and carry me to the other side of the locker area. Every day was just as hilarious but also meaningful.

As with Angie, Andrew and I shared many private jokes that stitched our friendship together. At one of my many house parties, Andrew decided to make the grandest of entrances into my bedroom by running and jumping onto my bed, which resulted in one leg breaking and my bed ending up lopsided. From then onwards I had to sleep in the middle to avoid rolling off, but all Andrew said was, "Now going to sleep is like an adventure." I could often rely on him to find the positive in every seemingly miserable situation.

His sense of humour was second to none, mainly because of his wit. And he was never afraid of whether a joke would embarrass him or not. He arrived at my house after school one day and when my mom asked him what he had been up to recently, his response was, "Oh, you know, I got my nipples pierced recently and I also got a tattoo, but I can't show it to you because it's in a bit of an awkward spot."

My parents admired and appreciated this kind of gutsy humour because they hadn't come across it in any of my other friends. Andrew was capable of making literally any person laugh.

Another instance occurred when our circle of friends came over to my house because Tim had agreed to make cheesecake for us—something he had been bragging about for ages. We had asked him to finally make the damn thing, and we were in the kitchen when Andrew decided to pick me up with his arms wrapped around my waist. He pressed on my stomach and I farted. In the kitchen. Surrounded by my favourite people. With a cheesecake in the oven. This rather smelly event turned into the trophy of insider jokes about our friendship. When it happened, I laughed uncontrollably, and whenever we spoke about it thereafter, endless giggles ensued. At least he said my fart sounded cute, something like a 'poot' sound.

Stomach gas aside, Andrew made me feel incredibly special when I thought the hierarchy was getting to me. He made me feel like I wasn't just another girl he had become close to, because we maintained a close friendship long after I left Saudi. He remained one of those friends who was always true to me in all the necessary ways. Andrew would never do wrong to anyone and never spoke behind anyone's backs without good reason.

Andrew was not attractive, but he was goofy and really smart—ideal criteria for the hierarchy to use as ammo in their bullying tactics. People who knew him knew how wonderful he was and what a fantastic friend he could be, but none of the hierarchy cared to see these attributes. It really hurt to watch because, being the 'popular one', standing up for him would mean denting my reputation, and I was too much of a coward to put that on the line.

What if I came in the firing line, too?

I watched the Arab boys insult him and pick his character apart and then laugh about it, and it made my insides burn. In my opinion, they were missing out on getting to know someone with a contagious positivity and epic sense of humour.

I never really found much in common with most of the Arabs of my year, except for some of the girls and a few of the guys. I often found that, when I did happen to get close to them, I was sucked into a portal of trouble and drama. After my past experiences I decided to stick to those who I was certain had my best interests at heart, not in a discriminatory way, but more in a selective manner that kept me guarded. But then I met Bilal.

Bilal couldn't have been more different to any of the other Arabs I had met or mingled with. He was from Syria and took great pride in this—I always admire someone greatly if they love where they come from— so we had something in common. Bilal was loved by everyone, but also feared by many, as he was known to work out in the gym most days and had arms like tree trunks. He may have looked tough and could certainly act that way, but one look into his green-blue eyes and you knew his soul was gentle and calm. He and I became incredibly close friends in year ten when he joined our form room, the year where it felt like all the dust was settling and my life was in order. He ultimately joined Angie and me in making a mockery of our form teacher, among many other childish but hilarious escapades.

If Bilal's buttons were pressed in the wrong way, he had a hidden side that could get particularly nasty. What I loved about him was that he never initiated any tension and made sure it stayed out of our friendship. Despite the differences in our upbringing and cultural background, we were very alike, and I admired his confidence in standing out as someone unique. We made each other laugh all the time; he was one of the most optimistic, positive people I knew back then.

On one of our Duke of Edinburgh expeditions we were required to follow a map around a section of a desert (imagine that) as a group. It was our last trip, so we had to get it right. We ended up getting horribly lost and had to break the rules in order to find our way back, so Bilal went to ask some children in a Bedouin tent for directions. Angie had a natural way of taking charge and being our leader (of myself, Bilal and Andrew) and of course got frustrated that we were stuck under the sun in the middle of the desert. Bilal sensed everyone's irritation and attempted to lighten the mood by saying everything in (what he perceived to be) a British accent. I could not contain my laughter—the result of a concoction of exhaustion, overheating, and my sincerely funny friend. Angie, the only one with a British accent in our group, took offence, but I think she found a small amount of amusement in his attempts to not let the group get grumpy. But thank goodness we had him to speak in Arabic to the desert dwellers who, thankfully, pointed us in the right direction.

Long after I left Saudi, Bilal and I remained very close friends. He had a magical way of transforming from class clown to the friend I needed to lean on. Sure, we had our disagreements and viewed the world slightly differently, but he was like my big, protective brother who I wanted around me all the time. I know he had a small crush on me at one point, but this passed quickly. I think (I hope) he realised that we had something special and sacred so that, should teenage feelings intervene and the dynamic change as a result, it would be a real pity. I admired him so much as someone with a strong mind and strong heart, certain of who he was in all spheres of life.

Sean was another character who I had enormous respect for. He was a quirky individual who was an awesome friend to me. Another incredibly smart person, he combined his intellect with his unique sense of humour to produce hilarious remarks while still loving those he cared for dearly. Like Angie, he was one of my more mature friends, which I found intimidating when we first interacted. But, by the middle of year ten, he and I grew closer and the intimidation faded. Sean was also, unfortunately, the target of snide comments from the top of the hierarchy because he was short and had, apparently, a large forehead. Luckily, none of these comments seemed to affect who he was as a clever and remarkable person. He took very little nonsense from the bullies, a characteristic I was envious of.

Adding to my initial intimidation were Sean's staggeringly blue eyes: he had the sort of eyes that made it difficult for a person not to give them their full attention, myself included. He always gave great advice, at school and for many years afterwards, and was one of my go-to people when I needed cheering up. Before our friendship grew deeper, I thought he didn't really care about my problems (because there were often many), or when he knew I was upset, but he proved me wrong many times. He was an excellent listener, so I always thought of him when I needed someone to talk to. Honesty was one of his primary attributes, which meant I could always depend on him, sometimes more than on others.

He and I were a fantastic team, both in our English class and outside. He had been in my English class for three years up until my exit from 'sand land', and we got in trouble almost every single lesson with our poor teacher, Mrs Bruce. I loved laughing with him, even if it meant risking Mrs Bruce's wrath, pulling funny faces at each other from across the room or sending each other cheeky notes. We could never be trusted to sit together quietly because it was difficult not to talk to him.

When I was looking for someone with whom I had mounds in common, it was Sean. We both appreciated the little things, something I struggled to find in other people who were more concerned with what was happening right in front of them. Sean and I had a deep curiosity about many things that made up what it means to be a human being, a shared interest that was rare between two teenagers. We shared passions and many special moments, big and small—like when we were on the Duke of Edinburgh trip and the sun was setting, and he invited me to sit on a rock with him to watch its descent. Up until then no one really cared what the sun was doing, except for Sean and me. That moment, as simple as it was, sort of sealed the envelope of our friendship and I wanted to do everything I could to make sure it remained airtight.

Somehow, Sean was moved to a seat in front of me in our English classes, sitting there right up until my farewell. We had a new teacher at the start of year eleven, as Mrs Bruce had left for Kuwait; the new teacher lived on my compound and we grew quite fond of him. I was sad to say goodbye to Mrs Bruce—a teacher who always pushed me to do better—but Sean and I took full advantage of the fact that the teacher was new, so we often put him to the test. He was a lot less picky with our academic work, which was a huge bonus and meant that my marks improved, but we then felt guilty for misbehaving in class. Sean introduced me to the harmless game of 'Would you rather…' which we mostly played during English. You might be wondering how one keeps a straight face when asked: "Would you rather lick a homeless man's toe, or kiss a pirate with scurvy?"

Fun and laughter were never in short supply with Sean. He was always upbeat, always tried to see the brighter side of things, and I couldn't help but smile whenever he was around. Sean and I's bond was one of those that went beyond the Saudi borders where he ended up coming to South Africa to visit me while I was in university, and we attended a festival together.

I had a few in between friends who came and went but still made a mark. Layla was one of them. Layla and I were the 'Africans' of the year and of Eid Compound, because she lived four doors down from me, because she came from Nigeria (but lived her whole life in London) and I, well, was a neighbour from further down south on the continent. Then we became close neighbours on the mutual ground of Riyadh, which provided some comfort as we were both away from our beloved continent of Africa. She and I were almost like sisters, albeit for a rather short period of time, but we had such similar mind-sets regarding how we thought about and processed things, whether it was schoolwork or a personal crisis. But deciphering Layla was a tiring exercise at times. Sometimes she decided she didn't want to talk to me. We sat next to each other on the school bus, with her little brother in between us, from the day she arrived at the school to my very last day, approximately two years in total. I would often sit down and say, "Good morning," and then just know she was not interested in a conversation. These periods would sometimes last for a week at a time and I was convinced that she thought I was annoying—why else would she decide to ignore me? However, when she chose to speak to me again, I was extremely excited, like an enthusiastic puppy. In hindsight this was probably a small manipulation tactic (whether she acknowledged it or not), because she knew I would do anything for her and would never confront her for being selective when it came to the times when she wanted to interact with me.

Layla and I, similar to my friendship with Angie, tried to avoid arguing at all costs because we hated how it made us feel. The majority of the friendship was spent helping each other, handing out advice on things that had happened to us. Also similar to Angie, she was straightforward with her thoughts, sometimes quite abrupt, and often it went a bit too far where I felt offended, rather than humbled, by her wise and honest advice (but this could be because of my fragile teenage soul). There were a few incidents when she was quite nasty to me, whether this was her intention or not, but I am glad those moments never defined our friendship. We grew incredibly close leading up to my end date in Saudi. Saying goodbye to her felt difficult and painful, because I thought she was going to be one of those friends that had inched closer and closer to a permanent spot in my heart. We simply did not have enough time together.

Although some friendships were fleeting, Ashleigh was a constant. She was, and still is, one of my most adored and precious friends that you simply cannot replicate. She is comprised of so much talent, bravery, originality, and loyalty—one of those friends you can let in on your deepest, darkest secrets and not a single ounce of judgement will flash across her eyes, and all ties of trust remain intact without a threat. Ashleigh was from San Antonio, with a Puerto Rican mother, and had been in Saudi a lot longer than I. She went to the American International School but lived on my compound. She was one of the first people I met when I spotted her playing goalkeeper during a soccer game on the basketball court behind my house at Eid, and I am so thankful for that.

Ashleigh was quite an introvert, but ironically had a huge circle of friends and was liked by everyone I knew. As our friendship solidified, bound by a mutual obsession with the likes of *A Day to Remember* and *My Chemical Romance*—soundtracks to the emo/gothic phase that we went through together, along with black rubber bracelets—I knew I had gained a friend who would stand beside me through every trial and would help me overcome them. When I wrote the first draft of this book when I was fifteen and wrote about Ashleigh, it had been two years and twenty-four days since I had last seen her. Since then, it has been more years and still too many days. But I hold her as close as if I saw her for the first time just yesterday on the soccer field.

Ashleigh left to go back to the United States a year after we met, and I was shattered. She was my go-to girl in the compound and I couldn't help but feel a sense of emptiness that she was now going to be on the opposite side of the world. But, as it went in Saudi, people left, and you had to find ways to move on. Ashleigh came back for a visit just under a year later and I was ecstatic to have her even for a short while, but then she told me that she was actually going to stay until further notice. This prompted the second phase of our friendship, and the best part of our story together.

What I loved about Ashleigh was that I knew I could always count on her, and she never forgot about me. At the time, I was having many doubts and issues with insecurity about my friendships because so many people had turned their backs on me. I always wondered if I was the problem and if there was something about me that acted as a deterrent. Ashleigh reassured me that there was nothing wrong with me, that she accepted me in all my awkward glory, and that she would never leave me. She had so many different friends from school and outside of school, yet she still called me on New Year's Eve, when I had just landed back in Riyadh after my December holiday in Johannesburg, to ask me how we were going to celebrate.

She also came to me when she needed help. I recall a day when she came to visit me at home, ran up the stairs to my room, closed the door, put her hands to her face and burst into tears. I had never seen her cry and it was heart wrenching. Her parents were getting divorced and, for obvious reasons, this was incredibly difficult to come to terms with.

Ashleigh was not like me when it came to boys and she seemed to have little interest in them altogether, but now, the only example of a romantic union that she knew had fallen apart. How does a fourteen-year-old tell her friend that everything is going to be okay when the people who had known her the longest, loved her the longest, were choosing to go their separate ways? I felt so inadequate at that moment, but I don't think she was looking for someone to tell her what to do next, or the best way to react, because there was no best way. She just needed *someone*. Someone who wouldn't judge, who would take her vulnerability in that moment seriously, and respond the way a best friend should.

Ashleigh and I had many special times together, so many that we made a point of reminiscing about them whenever we Skyped after she moved back permanently to the United States. Saying goodbye to Ashleigh for a second time was one of the most heart-breaking things I had ever experienced at the time, because it felt like I was losing my left arm. Ashleigh wasn't overly emotional or overtly expressive but, like a left arm would, she kept me balanced, and she was one of those people whose words of insight, when I needed them, just stuck. She touched so many people and was such a phenomenal friend. She came to visit me in South Africa in 2012 which proved the value of our friendship and its cross-continental strength, and it has remained exactly the same ever since. We have both been through a lot since then, but we always make a point of sending each other a message every once in a while. She has become one of those people whose friendship does not require constant communication for it to remain steadfast, but rather requires the trust and faith that we both still love each other and that our friendship is permanently ingrained into our minds.

So, there were the Angies and Andrews and Ashleighs of my life, alongside the Laylas and Bilals, and there were so many in between. Up until the moment I left, I was so happy about who was surrounding me—this fearless little community of friends that made me laugh and kept me upright. A few I hadn't mentioned were no less.

Tariq was a boy living on Eid and an integral part of our circle, wowing us all with his amazing skills on the soccer field as well as his ability to fit in with the older kids despite being two years younger. He and I became incredibly close, sharing long phone calls at the end of the day, and I had to be reminded often that he was not my age. He was so bright and so kind and so caring, and I am very glad we became close friends.

Then, at school, there were the Simos and the Mahids, the Harrys and the Toms and the Dees, the Sandras and the Marahs—all individuals who made coming into school a less daunting experience. Who focused on the good surrounding them and who paid less attention to how they could bring others down to make themselves appear more superior. Who loved looking at life the way that I did.

I will forever be grateful that I could take these relationships with me when I left. Sure, we have all gone our separate ways and had to accept, eventually, that there was always going to be another life waiting for each of us after Saudi. But the lucky thing about all of this is that no one can take away the memories or the appreciation we had for one another — Saudi has bound us forever, I think. These relationships were tried and tested, and tested dozens of times thereafter, and some did not pass. But the ones that did are the ones that stay with me and I remember them with fondness. Always.

CHAPTER SIX
Goodbye, and Hello

It felt like the dust of just over two years of torment, embarrassment, hurt, betrayal, and questioning had finally settled. I had established a fantastic, solid group of friends. I was back on my feet—with my family and friends helping me to stay on them—and the people who I felt had enjoyed a path of terrorising others for a bit too long had themselves been visited by karma. Harriet became the butt of many jokes as she continued to try to assert herself as an overly confident, boy-wrangling presence in our year of students accompanied by a 'screw you' attitude, only to find this kind of behaviour was not received well by those around her. Rudwan's true colours were revealed (although I had already seen them long before) to the lower members of the hierarchy who wouldn't stand for his conniving, impure approach to adolescent life. His journey at our school seemed to have come full circle. He was back to where he started as the boy from Pakistan that people made fun of, and was largely unaccepted by his peers. Others, however, continued to squash those who threatened their self-perceived superiority, so people like Nader were established as the ringleader of the hierarchy, and often seen with a trail of frightened minions behind him.

Although I was somewhat pleased that the people who shattered the, admittedly, very thin veneer of how I perceived myself—along with many other poor young individuals attempting to establish a footprint on this planet—had faced some sort of consequence to their actions, there was, remarkably, a small part of me that felt bad for them. Ever since I was young, I had never been an 'I hope you rot in hell' kind of person, and never wished misfortune on anyone despite how they may have wronged me. And, in a confusing way, I had true empathy for the people, two in particular, who apparently had very little for me. I have also always believed there is a plan for each one of us about the hand that is dealt us, so I found comfort in knowing that life had this handled, whether it was to be then or further on down the line, for the people who made me feel like I had very little substance. Along with this, I struggled to keep all the pieces of my fragile identity together. But at the end of the storm—the online bullying, the real-life bullying, the disloyalty—I felt more together than I had in years.

It was just a normal school day when I arrived back at our villa in Eid to see my mom and dad standing in the kitchen, my dad in casual clothes rather than his usual work attire. I was excited to see my dad home early but also puzzled as to why he was not still at work.

They noticed my confusion and announced that our lives were about to change again.

"Quite simply, Gabriella, we have just got ourselves a one-way ticket out of Saudi Arabia. I will not be working for Al-Rajhi Bank any longer and we are moving back home to South Africa," my dad explained.

My thoughts were everywhere, my emotions went haywire, and I wasn't sure how to react. So I broke down in a bout of ugly sobbing laced with notes of resentment as, just as I hadn't been ready to leave South Africa for a foreign country in 2007, I was even less prepared to uproot my life again, especially now that I had just started to love my life in this dusty city.

I tried to negotiate with them and explain that things were finally going well for me, that I had eventually established a group of friends I was convinced were going to be with me forever, that my academics were stable and that I had just figured out who I was as a young person, with dreams and passions and goals. And that they couldn't do this to me, not now anyway. I was not ready.

I was also concerned about what this meant for my schooling career as it was December 2010, midway through my final year of GCSEs, and I was due to write my final exams the following June. This was totally disruptive and I wondered, for a moment, whether my parents had my best interests at heart as they said they did.

Why couldn't we just stay until I had finished my exams, when the end was supposed to be? Why couldn't we just stick to the plan?

I was, yet again, heavily resistant to another change. A different kind of stubbornness and irrationality and unwillingness to understand the rationale behind this news washed over me, and I was devastated. It was different to when my parents announced our move to Riyadh from Johannesburg when I was twelve because, since then, I had experienced so much that had moulded who I was in that moment: love, pain, friendship, and everything else in between. My identity had undergone multiple stresses and upliftment and traumas, completely separate from my past life in Johannesburg, which now felt so distant.

As soon as the news had sunk in, I immediately told my boyfriend, Akeem, that I was leaving. Still an attention-seeking, heartbroken teenager, I announced to all those closest to me that they would no longer see me on the soccer field or in the classroom, and that my chapter in Riyadh was coming to a premature end. The messages of support and expressions of sadness and disbelief came in their masses and, though I wished it were under different circumstances, I was reassured that I was, in fact, loved. And that, according to what I was reading, I was going to be missed. At that point I reflected that I had incurred many dents in myself owing to all the events associated with my time in Saudi. But they had slowly begun to heal thanks to the incredible people surrounding me, and now I was the one leaving a hole by announcing my imminent departure from a country that had crept its way into a sacred crevice of my heart.

I then wanted to know the plan.

When would we be leaving, what about my exams, what about my dad's employment?

We were leaving in three weeks from that day. My sister and I would be going to a British College in Johannesburg that offered Cambridge exams, and my dad would remain unemployed until the next right job found him.

The following three weeks felt like a blur, as I had to start to come to terms with the fact that most moments from then on were going to be critical.

Remember, Gabi, you cannot visit Saudi ever again. Make these moments count.

In those last few weeks—and this was only realised with the benefit of hindsight, so many people who were either mere acquaintances, distant friends, friendly classmates, or people who were mutual in all the drama that took place because of the perceived powers of the hierarchy—I realised I was not an ordinary character in my school's narrative. I had a presence that people would miss, meaning they felt it in the first place. This I gathered from people I didn't usually talk to, both in my school and outside of it, who sent me messages saying that I would be missed, that they wished they had taken the time to get to know me, that it was a shame my departure was so abrupt. I wondered, then, where these people had been all this time, when all I wanted was reassurance that people simply wanted me around and that my suffocating insecurities were nothing more than illusions, that I had created myself.

Why was it that it took an announcement of my forever-goodbye for people to come forward and give me the friendship and camaraderie I craved, and had been so desperate for, all this time?

But I couldn't ponder all these questions for which I knew I couldn't get answers, and will probably never know the answers to. Maybe it was one of those classic situations where you never really knew what you had until it was gone—that I was this addition to the collective that made people comfortable and happy. I was also so affected by my discomfort in my own skin that, perhaps, this adoration and acceptance was there the whole time and I hadn't realised because it was all overshadowed by trauma. Nonetheless, although it occurred in such a short period of time, I was elated to know that I had made a mark and that my title of 'school snitch' was no longer on everyone's lips. And that maybe, despite the fact that the events that took place would remain with me forever and determine my path from then onwards, I had been a constant contributor in people's lives rather than a fleeting figure in a tartan skirt in the school corridors that people would quickly forget. It also reassured me that the people I had taken the time to invest in, to laugh with, to listen to, were reciprocating.

The days went on, and the reality of the end of my time in Saudi grew nearer while the anchor on my heart grew heavier. I spent most of my last few nights leaving puddles of tears on my pillows because I was not ready to leave this home I had made for myself. That my parents had made for us. That my friends were a part of. That my memories were embedded in. I was dating a boy I adored, who treated me like a queen, and who expressed nothing other than devastation when he knew my departure was getting closer. I was in a happy place. And there was nothing I wanted to do to prepare myself to leave all of that behind because I was in so much denial and disbelief that my miniature kingdom was going to dissolve in a matter of weeks. My final week arrived and I remember going into school, for every day of that week, with a giant lump in my throat.

The weekend before, however, I had plans to visit Angie at her compound with a few other friends. Now that I knew time was a precious asset, I made sure to never miss a minute with her. She signed me in (the standard, rigorous security procedure upon entering every compound) and we walked to her house so I could put down my bag. My love for taking photographs had started as soon as my mom taught me how to use a camera, so I had my camera around my neck but not much else. Angie told me we were going to meet some of her compound friends at a recreation centre. I was initially confused, but followed her lead anyway. We entered this dingy room I had never been to previously, and before I could register what was happening a group of about thirty of my friends came out of nowhere yelling, "Surprise!"

I had seen others being thrown surprise birthday parties and the like, and often got upset because no one had ever thought to do that for me. But there I was, standing in a room of people who wanted to be there without me asking them to be, looking at the hardest thing I was going to be leaving behind: my people. The year before that, in February, Ashleigh had thrown me a surprise party for my birthday, with many of the same people present. I was then, as now, completely awash with disbelief that these people were there for me and me alone, combined with adoration for the people who considered me worthy of such a farewell (and went through the stress of rallying together a group of fifteen-year-olds and getting them to co-operate). It was none other than Angie and Bilal behind it all, and I consequently had a smile plastered on my face for days afterwards. There was, in the end, no anti-climax for me—this party assured me that I was loved and that I would be leaving with a heart filled to the brim.

The final days were drawing closer, and with them came an increasingly sore heart. And then the last day arrived like a ton of bricks. I walked out through the school turnstiles wedged between thick, concrete walls—there to protect us from the non-Western world and to separate us from them—and got on the school bus back to Eid for the very last time. My baby blue, collared school shirt was adorned with messages written by my friends in permanent marker, a souvenir for me to take away and read when nostalgia visited. I couldn't believe I wasn't going to be seeing most of these people ever again.

My last week at school also marked the last week for everyone else as the December holidays were commencing. The night before we were due to leave, a whole bunch of my friends came to my compound to say their farewells, including people I had not known for very long who still wanted to see me off. My boyfriend, Akeem, was by my side the whole time, fully aware that his 'Tweety'—the nickname gifted to me by him because of my chubby, smiley cheeks—was being taken away from him by the Saudi powers that dictated our very belonging in the country. My dad, who was angry I had stayed out for longer than expected, interrupted our last hug and kiss goodbye. But I reasoned that any goodbye under any circumstances would feel incomplete, because there would always be something more you would want to do or say in that final moment. There was no such thing as a perfect goodbye when that goodbye initiated years and years of distance with no sign that you would ever be able to see the person again or that the distance would close. This fact made it all so much more difficult. I felt this not only with Akeem, but with Tim, Angie, Bilal, my Eid family, Andrew, and several others who gave Saudi so much more meaning and substance for me—a chapter I would carry in my pocket for the rest of my life.

***

We flew back to South Africa the next day, and images of our empty villa are still fresh in my mind as I write this. Although our villa was identical to the one next door, and the one next door to that, villa 190 housed not only us as a family, but also my memories, my secrets, my heartaches, and my fondest feelings. All that was left was the ugly compound furniture that came with the villa, stains in the carpets from spilled drinks, and my signature etched into my bedroom door for its next inhabitant to decipher. We had several big, hard-shell suitcases accompanying us back to our home country as we all piled into a mini-bus—the only transport that was big enough for our haul. My mom asked the bus driver to take a photo of us, marking the last time we would ever be seen in Eid. At the back, in the darkest corner, you can just make out a young Gabi with a desperate, tear-stained face, so unwilling to leave those gates for a final time. I looked like I was grieving someone's death given how out of control my emotional reaction was, but I guess that's what it felt like at the time. This was the only time I didn't want to go back home to my own country.

By the time we arrived at the airport, my wailing had dissipated as I was simply overcome by exhaustion and numbness. I was spotted by a classmate at the airport on his way back to Algeria for his December holiday, who I said another goodbye to, and then my family and I boarded the plane. My dad's bank at least had the courtesy to send us off in the comfort of first class—the same way we had arrived. I don't think I even caught a final glimpse of Riyadh at night because my eyes were tired and stinging from crying, and so Riyadh and I never got to lock eyes again as we ascended into the dusty, dark sky to our next temporary house in our forever home country.

Landing back in Johannesburg, everything felt the same and relatively normal—like I had not just bid farewell to four years in an alien country that shaped who I ultimately became. But maybe this was a good thing and I accepted that I would be able to deal with the reality of not returning to Saudi. For then, I had to handle all the busyness that every December holiday brought for us.

I remember feeling rather out of sorts after being back in my home country, South Africa, for a few days. I woke up every day to, firstly, sharing a bedroom with my sister, followed by greenery outside, a blue sky, and little restriction on how we moved around Johannesburg and no need to put on an abaya when leaving the house. But what was the point of having all this freedom when my heart belonged somewhere else? I was still talking to Akeem daily, we were still dating because we hated the thought of a label that wasn't 'together', despite the fact that we were continents apart and unlikely to see each other ever again (silly, and naïve, I know). I was still scrolling through pictures of my final times in Saudi like they were the last pictures I would ever be allowed to take on Earth. I was still making sure that I knew about all the goings-on of life post-Gabi in Saudi, still involving myself in gossip and rumours and banter with my lifelong friends as if my return was around the corner. But I struggled to come face-to-face with the fact that Saudi and I were inevitably going to grow apart—this was imminent either by distance or by sentiment. I had ultimately been forced to divorce myself from a place and a community that I, at the time, couldn't see myself without. And I was now being thrown back into a different way of living, a different pool of people, and had to teach myself to swim again.

Re-integrating into my circle of friends who were still in Johannesburg was surprisingly seamless. I had to remind myself that they were also navigating the windy roads of adolescence just as I was, except our experiences were set against completely different canvases. I was not superior to them, although the fact that I had lived in a foreign country and travelled a lot made me feel like the lenses of my eyes were slightly more developed. Moving to a different country and experiencing different cultures certainly made my young horizons more elastic. Looking back now, however, I felt like I was the different one because of my well-travelled young life and that my old friends—who, when I left, were just children, but were now outspoken teenagers—might've viewed me (at that time) as if I walked around with my nose in the air simply because I thought I had to more to offer than they did. Not because I was *better* than them, but because I had merely experienced a lot more than the average teenage South African had at that stage in life.

Was I to blame at all? How could I control how I projected myself if the most critical moments of my adolescence took place in a totally different environment to theirs?

Despite this, we had a lot in common. We all wanted to rebel. Sleepovers at my friend Kayleigh's house involved sneaking in vodka coolers and trying to smoke cigarettes on the balcony, only for us all to choke as the smoke caught the backs of our throats, and playing drinking games outside on her patio despite it being a cold winter in Johannesburg. The one thing everyone else was doing that I wasn't was getting fake IDs and going clubbing. This they did with their parents' knowledge out of fear that their child might be ostracised for not doing what all the other kids were doing. My parents, however, would not budge, even if it meant their daughter being isolated from the rest of what the cool kids were doing on the weekends. The closest I got to this act of rebellion was going to a house party where the invite went viral across the suburbs of

Johannesburg, in a rented house in a questionable area of the city, packed to the walls (topped with electric fences) with young people dying to make something exciting of their weekends, only for it to be shut down by the police a few hours later. I couldn't even try explaining an event like this to my friends in Saudi who were still having fun, but controlled, evenings around the compound pool with their parents' homebrew and music on a small Bluetooth speaker.

Our living situation in Johannesburg was far from desirable. We bought a lock-up-and-go townhouse in Fourways, a stone's throw away from the home where I grew up, that had only served to house us when we were visiting from Saudi—but we now had to live in it until further notice. Transitioning from a four-bedroom, spacious villa in a compound, where you could play a game of soccer or go for a swim whenever you felt like it, was not easy. I was now sleeping in a bunk bed with my sister, my parents in a tiny room with a cubbyhole en-suite bathroom, and a shared study that doubled as a laundry room. We lived in a complex that had the character and atmosphere of a doctor's waiting room, with strict rules pertaining to pets that could not be bigger than a ruler and, should you even dream about renovating, then your house had to fit the exact aesthetic guidelines outlined by the complex. The irony was that all the houses looked the same, but so did all the villas in Saudi, and yet somehow this felt more clinical and even more controlled in comparison to the extreme fundamentalism that existed in our old country in the Middle East. There was a severe lack of life compared to my previous compound.

It didn't take me long to fit back in. I may have had all these worldly experiences that placed me five steps ahead of my peers, but it was incredibly refreshing and comforting to return to people that were like me. They valued what I did and treated others in the same way I did. Unlike in Saudi, where my identity and sense of self constantly felt under threat, being back in South Africa reassured me that there was a community of people that accepted me and loved me for who I was. In fact, it was almost as if I had carried my status of being 'popular' across continents, as this exact title was appended to me when I settled into the British International College in Bryanston, where I was due to complete my final GCSE exams.

Starting at another new school was an additional challenge I had to overcome. The British International College, otherwise known as BIC, was not a conventional college. It was a small building that simply served as a base for around two hundred students aspiring to obtain internationally recognised secondary school certificates. There were rumours that the college was once a home for psychiatric patients. The leadership was shocking, and everyone I knew scowled at the principal who drove home at lunch time in her Mercedes Benz while we sat on broken benches and had nothing but a basketball court for any outdoor activity.

I soon came to acknowledge that this was just a physical space for me to write my exams. In just eight months' time I would be heading off to boarding school in England, so I entered the school with the end already in sight, with very little intention of putting effort into establishing a social life (because I already had one with my old friends, so didn't think I needed anyone else). This was partly because I had now been thrown into a band of misfits and weirdos who I judged immediately, and because I was still bitter and heartsore at being apart from my special people all the way back in Riyadh. Akeem and I were still dating, at that point.

I rapidly learned that I was not the type of person to deny myself a group of friends that I could rely on, misfits or not. I acknowledged that I, too, was a misfit. My ideals and romantic view of the world were not attributes commonly found in many fifteen-year-old girls in Johannesburg. But anyway, I quickly established a group of friends—an odd mixture of people with varying backgrounds and tastes in music, who were already miles ahead of me when it came to weekend activities. It had been made crystal clear to me by my parents that, should I go to a party where alcohol was present, I was only allowed three drinks that didn't contain any spirits (Hunters Gold was my drink of choice). I was not allowed a fake ID and I was not allowed to go anywhere unfamiliar to my parents. But here I was, spending time with people I actually grew to love, who smoked cigarettes, weed, did tequila shots, and who were generally allowed free rein over whichever turf they chose to explore. I quickly learned that there was a sad lack of family and shelter in their lives in comparison to mine, and that they took care of themselves most of the time.

It might sound snobby, but I felt like my sister and I were the only people with comparatively normal lives at BIC. Our peers were only sent there for the Cambridge exams and little else, with parents who didn't have much investment in their lives. The only parallel I could draw with Saudi was that, although in a different way, BIC attracted students from all over Africa. And so I was integrated into my second international batch of individuals. There was Vaughn from Cote D'Ivoire, Katarina from Serbia, Ben and Lily from England, and the rest from different corners of Johannesburg and Africa. It may have been that these people were not like the ones I grew to adore in Saudi, but I didn't shy away from finding out about them or choose to isolate myself because of who I was in comparison to who they were. I was surrounded by people that had every reason to feel bitter about life and the hand they were dealt. But they had nothing but pure intentions and, actually, just wanted to feel bound by *something,* even if it was a friendship with a community of youngsters that was joined by both everything and nothing at all.

I mentioned my supposed popularity in this new environment; I was unsure how to react to it. In Saudi, my popularity was a result of my appearance and background, and it seemed like there was not much more to it than that. These reasons also did not stop the tyrannical, bullying behaviour of some in Saudi, so my status was not necessarily something I relished, because I was aware it was not something I had earned or had to cherish as a means of protection from those deemed more superior. But back in Johannesburg, there was something more honest in the way I was perceived. People didn't spread rumours, no one bullied me, and I recall being taken aback when a girl in the grade below me came up to me at lunchtime to tell me that she thought I was beautiful. I had been called beautiful by a few people in Riyadh, but this felt so much more authentic. For the first time in four years, I was not scared of walking into school and I was unthreatened by the people around me. However, this did not diminish the fact that my confidence and self-esteem were still in tatters, and I was clueless as to how to start stitching it all back together. I wondered, just because my environment felt more positive and more conducive to lifting me up, if it meant my anxious thoughts and insecurities should have reason to flee. At BIC I had many admirers and I could feel eyes on my backside as I walked up stairs—I definitely knew that I was an attractive presence in a very drab establishment—but the flattery was not enough to squash the thoughts that I still wasn't enough.

I had established two groups of friends at this point: those from my old school and those from this new, temporary school. While both groups were similar ages and on similar paths through life, it became glaringly obvious how different they were from each other. It was essentially a group of people from great backgrounds and upbringings at one of the best schools in the city (my previous school), next to another group of misfits thrown together from differing environments. My old friends tried, but in the end, I was the only thing the two groups had in common. I learned this about myself: how, despite being surrounded by people with polar opposite upbringings and beginnings to mine, I still looked for—and found—the things I liked most about them, which would mean we could establish a relationship. Given how little BIC cared about the wellbeing of its students and did nothing to invest in them, I gathered we all needed each other anyway.

BIC was small. There were only around two hundred students in total, so you had to find friends fast before all the good ones were taken. I was totally disinterested in making friends when I arrived for my first day, knowing I was just there to finish the subjects necessary for writing my exams. But friends found me when a bubbly girl named Kelly, with a strange American twang, came up to me at break time to ask me to sit with her and a few others. I sat down and was introduced to a brother and sister from England and their cousin, who also had a strange American twang, but who was very pleasant. Before I knew it, these people, this mismatched group of strangers, had crept into my heart and I created an honest, genuine friendship with them. We were joined later by two other boys, considered nerds, but with the most loving and caring hearts, and not an ounce of discrimination or judgment existed amongst us. Compared to the toxicity that surrounded me in Saudi, this was all incredibly refreshing.

The irony was that BIC had a reputation amongst other elite schools in Johannesburg and people would wince, like they had just bitten into a lemon, when you told them the name of the school you were attending. There was a strong classist attitude among people from other schools, perpetuated by teenagers, despite the fact that the curriculum at BIC was much stronger. So the inhabitants of BIC lived carefree lives, respected others and avoided judging one another, but, from the outside, they were the ones being judged.

Man, I hate teenagers.

Not that I was looking, but the prospects of boys that I could potentially crush on at BIC looked pretty dismal. There was one cute, blond boy who I took a liking to, after Akeem and I realised the heart-breaking reality of never being able to see each other again and decided to end things. He seemed to like me, too. He appeared to be more similar to me in terms of our upbringing but, mainly, he was *the only* cute blond boy in the school. He and I started talking and even had secret meetings in the school storeroom to steal kisses, and I liked holding his hand, but there was something about him I wasn't quite getting. I didn't feel entirely comfortable around him and thoughts of him didn't keep me up at night as most teenage crushes do. He also came across as sly and insincere, and I felt like he was using me to brag to his friends that he had managed to bag the new, hot girl. It was then that my instincts led me to discover that he actually had a girlfriend outside of school, something he tried to deny and lie about, and for once I was not convinced or manipulated by another teenage boy and broke things off as quickly as they had started. His reaction to me ending things (after probably a whole two weeks) was pathetic and childish, and I realised how above boys of his kind I was at that point. I felt like I was starting to regain some power and confidence of my own. He and his girlfriend are still together to this day.

At the time, I had a superiority complex that resided in my subconscious because of my station in life compared to that of my peers. Whenever I got close to someone at BIC, I felt as if I was taking in a lost puppy—like saying, "Here you go, this is what it feels like to be cared for and noticed." But this initial feeling went away when I realised, I needed them too. I became incredibly close with a tall black boy who seemed to care about the same things I cared about—the finer details, the smaller intricacies of life, what it means to be alive. We would have long phone calls every week and we even went to have milkshakes a few times, and I grew to adore him. He made me feel incredibly special and, no matter how many people I got close to at that school and how many of them faded, he was always constant, even beyond BIC. I seemed to cling to people that made me feel worthy and recognised, because it wasn't something I felt from people very often. He was different to me, though, and we didn't quite understand each other's lifestyles. His father died when he was young and he had a fragmented relationship with his mother. He was pretty much left to roam the world on his own and, while he was fiercely independent, he didn't have it all figured out and got in trouble sometimes. He was drinking hard liquor most weekends and experimented with drugs, while I was sipping on my prescribed three Hunters Golds on my patio with my friends. But these differences were not enough to divide him and I, and he remained an essential person in my life for a very long time. He still is, and we relish the fact that people have disappointed us so much over the years, but that we will always have each other.

Eight months passed, and I had written my final GCSE exams. I knew this was coming, we all did, but it didn't make it any easier. It was incredible how, in such a short space of time at such a dreadful place, I now struggled to tear myself from the connections I had made. And we knew it wasn't going to be a 'we'll keep in touch and we'll see each other again when you visit' kind of scenario. I was going to boarding school in

England, a decision finalised when we were still in Saudi, so there was an inevitability to all of it. But this meant saying another goodbye and my chest hurt because of it. This small community of weirdos that I had grown to love were a fantastic splash of colour when all I had been anticipating was eight months of grey. Everyone signed my shirt—a third shirt I could add to my collection—and I had to suppress a lump in my throat as I walked out of those gates for the last time. There went another school and group of people that were a part of my life when it was suitable, and would soon fade away when our lives went in different directions.

When my exams ended, I threw a party. By this I mean I had my five or six friends over to our tiny townhouse to sit around a fire and celebrate the fact that I now only had two more years of school to go (I was still subscribing to the British system with my school year ending in June, while my friends' year ended in December). We threw my exam notes and test papers in the fire because I was extremely relieved to be saying goodbye to eight months at the worst school I had ever been to—a school that cared nothing for its students or their success, and where my sister was in tears several times a week because she could not manage the social or academic scene. I was still a relatively happy person because I looked past all these issues and was admired by many, but my sister was still young and struggled to find people with whom she had anything in common. I was, unfortunately, completely oblivious to the fact that she was struggling, too caught up in my own mini-fame, so I wish I could've helped her more. But thankfully, this was a temporary period for her and one which she seems to have blocked out entirely.

A week before I was due to leave for boarding school in the UK, I hosted a farewell party with all my weird and wonderful friends. The differences between the two groups became even more apparent as the BIC kids sat in a circle, smoking cigarettes while the others stood in a close circle sipping on their vodka coolers (or nothing at all). One who arrived high got the greenies and ended up vomiting all over the clubhouse we had hired, and another resorted to vomiting in the bushes because she'd had one too many Smirnoff Spins. My other non-smoking, better-behaved friends silently watched and judged. Regardless of these differences, I loved both groups in different ways and was not embarrassed. And saying goodbye to them all was still really hard.

It was time for us all to go our own ways, and mine just happened to be over the big pond to the UK. I looked forward to starting at Malvern College, a school that offered the International Baccalaureate and was rated in the top ten for its academic programme. This was my choice over remaining in South Africa for boarding school at St Anne's Diocesan School, a place I refused to attend because: (a) it was an all-girls school and I didn't think I could cope being surrounded by all those hormones every day; (b) it had no soccer team; and (c) my mom went there and hated it, so I trusted her judgment. I wanted to remain in the British education system to avoid another heavy period of adjustment and I wanted my last two years of school to be the biggest bang of my schooling career.

And a bang it was. I just couldn't have anticipated how loud it was going to be.

CHAPTER SEVEN
Another New Arrival

The time had come for me to say 'see you later' to South Africa again, this time for a journey of my own making. It had, after all, been my decision to go to the UK, something I wanted and had chosen to do for the last two years of my schooling. But it was still hard to convince myself that this was indeed the right choice.

When we were still living in Saudi, we consulted with someone who knew the English educational system and the schools that would be most suitable for me, based on a cover letter that I had to write. A list of five top schools was compiled and we set off to England—just my mom and I—for our mini tour of what my academic future may look like. It was the most exhausting trip, but so much better than basing my decision off a script and photograph posted online or emailed to me.

I chose Malvern College in Worcestershire, partly because in the back of my mind I knew that Nick was already at a boarding school just over an hour away and that we may be able to see each other—a thought that lingered even after he left for boarding school and we broke up (those first loves bite you really badly).

Despite my time with Akeem and brief interludes with boys in Johannesburg, my feelings for Nick never fully went away as he was that first love that just stuck, so thoughts of being near him again excited me. But even more than that (for the first time a boy was not the overriding factor in my decision-making), Malvern College and I felt like a beautiful match. The school looked like Hogwarts; the lady who gave us the tour had spent a period of her life in Kenya; the head of sixth form, Mr Frayn, was from Umtali in Zimbabwe; the incoming housemistress of the boarding house I would go into was Mrs Swart from Rondebosch in Cape Town; and, to top it all off, Mr Antony Clark was the ex-headmaster of Bishops School in Cape Town and St Andrew's School in Grahamstown—the town I would later settle in for university—and the headmaster of Malvern College. Knowing I could be integrated into a mini, South African community, was incredibly comforting and one of the top selling points of the school for me (I highly doubt anyone else would consider these things). We had a meeting with Mr Clark, a true South African who just happened to find that life suited him better in England, and who was genuinely excited to welcome me to his school. I was immediately comfortable with him when I was in his office, and I later received a hand-written postcard from him, sent to me in Saudi, with the news that I had been accepted into the school, commencing September 2011.

Upon leaving Saudi, the only thing that felt certain was my move to the UK. I would be leaving behind four fantastic years and saying goodbye to special individuals—a traumatic upheaval—but my future academic life would be left unchanged. I guess I should have found some solace in this. But this was a weird parallel, considering I was so unprepared to close my chapter in Saudi but was forced to acknowledge that there was already another chapter waiting to begin. At least one thing was certain amongst all the unsuspecting curveballs flying our way.

The time came for my departure to the UK after a farewell to all my friends in Johannesburg. I was devastated to be saying yet another goodbye to them, but I had adopted an accepting mindset because I had made this decision for myself. I chose, at the age of fifteen, to finish off my schooling in the UK because I knew it was best, and that a lot could come from it when I was finished. I packed my bags and received a brand-new MacBook Pro laptop as the school had advised I get a Mac since the whole school operated on this system and "it would be easier." My whole family accompanied me to my new school. Ever since Tim had admitted his feelings to me over MSN Messenger and I discovered my delight at hearing this, we couldn't stop talking to each other and arranged to meet when I was in the UK. Although I was still strung up on Nick, I had to acknowledge that very little could come of us again, whereas there was a possibility with Tim. My family and I made a trip out of it, spending a few days in London, then heading to my mom's cousin and his wife—due to be my official guardians while I was in the UK—in a tiny town called Tewkesbury.

Tim, my best friend and now open admirer from Saudi, who was already settling into his boarding school in another county, met us. We decided to go for a walk down streets a lot stranger to me than they were for him; England seems to hold a familiarity for English people (he was from Liverpool) regardless of where in the country you are. While we were walking, he asked me if I would like to be his girlfriend. I questioned how such a relationship would work, considering he would be over two hours away and that we would both be going into new schools with strings attached. We agreed we would always be in touch and that he would visit me in Tewkesbury when it was our leave-out weekends. I was ecstatic that I was finally going to be hand-in-hand with my best friend after so many years of denying our spark. I almost breathed out an enormous sigh of relief, but this was short-lived. More about this later.

We arrived the day before I was due to move into my boarding house and all decided to take a walk around the campus before I settled in. I posed with Tim on the steps in front of the main building where we all revelled in the fact that this beautiful, history-rich school, packed with stories of C.S. Lewis and World War I, was going to be my home for the next two years.

We went back to our little hotel to talk about it. Tim and I had our first proper kiss. He got carried away and my boobs were seen and touched by a boy for the first time. My blood went cold, and the rest of my body followed. It happened so quickly; there was nothing gradual about the way he touched me and I didn't let it go any further. I told myself I just wasn't ready for anything of a sexual nature or for sex itself. The next time would be better. But I actually wasn't ready for anything with a boy, period. After so many years of being labelled a whore and a slut who had apparently slept with a boy ten months younger than me, I hadn't realised how untouched my body was until then.

After lugging huge, hard-shelled suitcases into Ellerslie House, followed by my equally heavy-hearted family, we began creating my little nook of a home in the boarding room I would be sharing with one other girl who hadn't arrived yet. Her name was Lisa and I felt that this story was going to be a happy one, since my best friend's name was also Lisa. That fact alone gave me an enormous amount of comfort. But Lisa would only be arriving the following day because of some kind of charity ball back in Munich that she had to attend with her family.

Saying goodbye to my family brought reality to a screeching halt. My heart sank as my mom's voice cracked and my dad's words quavered as they said goodbye. They left hastily to let me settle in and, essentially, rip off the Band-Aid. I then felt like I couldn't breathe. I sat on my little bed perched atop my storage drawers and wondered how the hell I was going to manage this.

You made this decision, Gabi, so get on with it.

I breathed in a breath that seemed to stem from my toes right into my lungs, closed my eyes, exhaled, and put on my armour. I was going to make this work and I was going to deliver good news to my family as often as I could. I hadn't realised it at the time, but I partially wanted to make my parents feel comfortable and relieved that their daughter was across the pond and happy about it. I met a girl from Nigeria—the first person I spoke to in my boarding house—who laughed at my jokes, so I thought I was off to a good start. Except the first joke included me accidentally spitting a piece of rice at her when we were having lunch, so at least my awkward self, remained intact, regardless of the country I was in.

Our boarding house had its own dining room, as opposed to central catering—the norm for the majority of boarding schools—which was where we had our introductory lunch. We shared a canteen with a boy's house, number seven, which was extremely progressive compared to most boarding schools in the world, never mind in England. Our housemistress, Mrs Swart, gave her welcome speech, and I was overwhelmed with excitement to hear another South African accent that I could access whenever homesickness kicked in. Remarkably, home was a distant thought at this point, and I was just looking forward to getting into a routine in this new environment that I now had to call mine. If I didn't take ownership, I would be facing a bitter, bumpy road ahead.

My German roommate finally arrived with her glamorous attire and bubbly demeanour. I was thrilled that she seemed excited to meet me, too. But it wasn't long before I realised that we were not going to be best friends like my other Lisa and me. She came from a totally different world to mine and I struggled to find anything that could connect us. She had a family home in Mallorca for weekend getaways from Germany, her brother was in the year above us and evidently a ring-leader—something I was familiar with, given the tyrants that used to dominate the hallways in Saudi—but which also meant she had immediate protection whenever she needed it. Her make-up was really nice and she looked a lot older than me. She was actually gorgeous. Our daily getting-ready routines revealed how little I knew about make up as I watched her put hers on—apparently you had to put mascara on *both* sets of eyelashes and not just the top ones.

The sixth form—the eldest two years of students—were not required to wear the school uniform. The dress code was a business suit, with some guidelines. We could wear make-up and heels (to a certain height) and our hair down, as long as it was clipped away from our faces. This was part of the enormous emphasis placed on treating us like adults because, essentially, that's what we were. In South Africa and Saudi, you could get detention for wearing BB cream or having a hair tie around your wrist. And here I was in England at the age of sixteen wearing a fitted ladies' Polo pinstripe suit.

As someone who had always found it easier to get along with adults, this kind of treatment suited me just fine. And it turned out I wasn't the only one comfortable in this environment as the majority of my peers all came from wealthy families who did not hold back when it came to the treatment of their children, almost as if they were on equal footing. Wearing suits and heels was not unfamiliar to them. They were all so experienced and mature that I felt like a child, despite my initial feelings of ease. But I tried my best to fit in despite my wavering confidence that I had made the right choice in coming here.

As the school filled up with all the new and existing students, it became apparent to me quite quickly that Malvern College had targeted a large German audience because of the reputation of the International Baccalaureate (IB) program, either as a marketing tactic or because of word of mouth. Like my parents, there was obviously a resounding commitment to giving their children the best education they could. While this was possibly one area of overlap between us, there was very little else that could initiate a close bond of similar values or common ground for me with any of the people at my new school. I felt immediately belittled and instantly different, and both these feelings stung. I had thought my days of being intimated by my peers were over.

My feelings of intense nervousness dissipated somewhat as soon as I met my teachers. The subjects I had chosen were English, Spanish and history at higher level (HL) and biology, economics and mathematics studies at standard level (SL). All respective departments had a fantastic team of educators. Clipped onto our IB subjects were theory of knowledge (ToK) and extended essay (a four-thousand-word essay on a topic of our choice), and CAS, a points system based on a creative activity, action-based activities, and a service (similar to the Duke of Edinburgh requirements). Compared to my previous years of schooling this new system seemed incredibly advanced, and I was concerned about how I would manage. Had I come straight from the South African education system I would have drowned within a month due to ill preparedness and spoon-feeding. Thankfully this wasn't the case as my British schooling in Saudi had prepped me adequately. It was the other aspects I wasn't ready for.

There was one facet of my life, unrelated to my move to the UK, that I needed to confront first. My now boyfriend, Tim, adored me. This was evident. There was a period when I felt exactly the same: excited that we had finally transformed our friendship into something more meaningful. I loved having someone who loved me as much as he did, and was not embarrassed to shout his feelings for me from the rooftops. But my feelings for him had begun to wane and I started to doubt my decision, wondering if this was what I really wanted. My emotions, and thoughts about breaking up with him, were confirmed when he came to visit me in Tewkesbury at my guardians' house during our first leave-out weekend. I knew as soon as I saw him get off the train when I collected him. That entire weekend was incredibly difficult for me, as I had made up my mind relatively quickly about my dissipating feelings for Tim, even when I tried to wait another day for my adoration for him to come flooding back.

Maybe you're just having an off day, I thought to myself.

I sat in the bathroom of my guardians' house in tears, wondering how I was going to make it through the weekend with this awful feeling sitting in my gut about the future of Tim's and my relationship. I felt like the worst person on earth, especially after he gave me a Liverpool FC jersey with my nickname and lucky number printed on the back. What I feared for the most, though, was that we could never go back to the fantastic friendship we had before we decided to be together. I knew what I needed to do and vowed to not force the relationship to continue or to lead him on for much longer. Decision-making was never my strong suit, but this incident was possibly the worst case of poor timing.

To illustrate how bad the timing was, and to add some tragic history to the context of the leave-out weekend, Tim's best friend Gareth, and one of my good friends from Saudi, was fighting a lengthy and gruelling battle against bone marrow cancer that had started in his ankle. Doctors in Saudi could not figure out what the problem was. In year eight, Gareth and his family returned to their home country of Canada, where his ankle pain continued. The Canadian doctors finally confirmed that he had bone marrow cancer and needed to be treated immediately. Treatment continued and he went into remission. But then he relapsed, and the doctors decided the safest option would be to amputate his leg to prevent the cancer from spreading. Tim visited Canada, and photos revealed a different version of our dear friend sitting on a boat with no hair and no leg. Regardless, he still had the same contagious smile. I am convinced that it was his optimism and larger than life attitude throughout this painful journey that kept him alive for so long.

A few days after my weekend with him, Tim phoned me to tell me that Gareth had died. Because he was such a fighter, even at the age of sixteen, I never thought the day would come. The cancer had spread to his lungs which were then filling up with fluid, and that's what eventually killed him. My grief and anger and pure heartbreak were overwhelming—I had no idea how to cope with this. And I had no idea how to comfort a boy who loved me and who I no longer loved in return.

Despite the awful news of the loss of our friend, I still knew I had to end things with Tim, which is what I did not long after the world lost someone so special to us, especially to Tim. I so badly wanted to be his best friend again, even though it was unfair of me to expect this. I felt heartless at the time given the circumstances, despite it being the right decision. Needless to say, Tim and I were never the same. We lost each other, and we also lost our friend.

***

We were all assigned a tutor who would be our mentor for our two-year journey through the IB. I was assigned Mrs Katie Adam, a petite, curly-haired blonde lady with the brightest smile I had ever seen. Like me, she was new to the school, but didn't seem new to mentoring as she made her role seem effortless. The connection between us was almost immediate and I was very quickly reassured that I would have someone in my corner when everything felt wobbly. She was my ultimate source of comfort and security and we agreed she would be my 'school mummy' throughout my time at Malvern. Like many others who cannot be without their mothers by their side, I couldn't have imagined Malvern without Mrs Adam. What was even better was that she was also my English teacher, so she helped me weather both my personal and academic priorities.

What became clear quite quickly was that all the teachers were genuinely invested in their students. They spoke to us like equals, they were always available when we needed help, and it was obvious that they loved walking into the classroom every day. They approached teaching with a certain finesse and care that I had never seen before, and this was an integral part of my experience which I carry with me to this day.

Malvern College was renowned not only for its academic programme but also for its sport. In our first or second week of starting school we were introduced to the various sports on offer in one of the halls in the main building. While walking around the hall I was only searching for the soccer sign-up sheet, which I couldn't find, until a sweet-looking girl named Nina came up to my circle and asked if anyone was interested in signing up for football (I later had to acquaint myself with calling it 'football' and not soccer). I shrieked with excitement and essentially ditched the girls from my house that I was with to put my name down and bombard Nina with questions. I now had something to keep me grounded and focused and excited: the sport that had remained my passion regardless of the country I was living in at the time, the sport where everyone was an equal on the field. I returned to my room with enormous eagerness for the first practice.

At that first practice session everyone was to be selected for the various teams, divided mainly by age groups and then by skill. Despite my initial excitement, it was incredibly difficult for me. I held back tears thinking about my old soccer team in Johannesburg and how the team shared a love and seriousness for the game that I simply could not see being replicated here in England. I felt like my last bit of hope of fitting in somewhere was gone.

But it wasn't long before we had a team like no other: the product of rigorous weeding-out of those who were either vaguely or half-committed, to result in the establishment of a collective of individuals who were determined to make their mark. We went on to become the team to beat, thanks to a fearless defensive line and a dominant attacking force. Aside from two or three other teams, we seized the ropes of women's football amongst schools in the south west and tugged until we had very little energy left. We fought properly for success in every single game and left our hearts on the field.

Mr Gauci, our coach, was shorter than me with a bald spot so shiny you could see your own reflection in it. He was head of history and a senior staff member, with a heart bursting with passion for our team, despite the fact that he had very little experience in playing the game itself. This did not matter, as he was undoubtedly an integral seam in the fabric of our team. His pride and enthusiasm and determination to see us through to success was so important and admirable that this trickled down to all of us, and the very same attitude became apparent in our team members. Without Mr Gauci, who often had us in hysterics in practice as he dashed through all of us on the field, our team would have simply been a group of individuals and not a team of people who shared the same love.

I am not sure how it happened, but five of us, myself included, were scouted to try out for the south west county schools' regional team. This was one of four provincial teams in the whole country. We made it through the trials and onto the team. While this was a massive milestone and a huge tick of self-assurance for me, my confidence, and lack thereof, got in the way. I was now thrown into a pool of sportswomen who were *all* good—I wasn't one of the outstanding few any more. The playing field was equal and a prime example of survival of the fittest. I struggled with this because it didn't feel natural; I was so used to leading the way instead of fitting in with the rest of the best, so I guess part of the experience was rather humbling. I battled to step up and show that I was worthy of being on the team, and struggled to deliver on my skill because I was so scared of messing up, so opted for a more conservative approach instead. Ultimately, this held me back and I only went to one south west training session. I also couldn't continue because my time in the UK had a deadline. But even if this weren't the case, I was afraid I might have cracked under the pressure despite this potentially being my ticket to my greatest dream of playing professionally. A lot of the girls I played with went on to play for the national schools' team and then on to the national under twenty-ones' side. That could have been me (South African passport aside).

In my final year at Malvern, I was determined to make the most of the time I had left, so I earned myself the position of captain of the women's first team football. I had never worn a title with so much pride. I went on to lead us to enormous success in our season and developed an unparalleled bond with the girls I mentored. Early mornings on the weekend, despite having to go to games and coming back late, didn't feel like a drag because I was truly doing the things I prized: leading others and playing a sport I loved with all my heart. Winning was the bonus. We travelled all across England to play against our opponents, even going to Rome for an international charity tournament in which we were highly placed.

Our record should have made people take us seriously, but this wasn't the case. When we played at home, very few came to support us, and I often had to deal with snide remarks from boys in my year, reminding me that, "Football is for guys, you know that, right?" But I had my own sense of pride when it came to my first love, even if I didn't for many other facets of my life, and they simply could not penetrate it or dampen or contaminate the thing that made my everyday life bearable. Others waited for a sunset atop the Malvern Hills; I waited for practice.

In one of our final chapel services, I was awarded full colours for football—an accolade I still carry with great pride. I may not have conquered playing for the south west team, but getting full colours was a very close second. The badge is still in my dressing table drawer.

Another of my titles I was proud of was that of peer mentor. I earned this as the result of thorough training to become qualified as a student who could mentor fellow students—either in my boarding house or outside—about whatever was on their mind. We covered the various topics of bereavement, bullying, and the ebbs-and-flows of puberty, and became knowledgeable in order to help others who may need support. We were like mini counsellors. This was a service option as part of our CAS programme where we had to fulfil certain hours and, while many others chose it as an easy way to obtain the necessary hours, I genuinely wanted to become a person, others could look up to, and who they could approach for help. The thing is, everyone at my school had such a thick veil of pride shielding them that they dared not let anything inflict a single chink in their armour. Vulnerability appeared to be something powerful enough to create that first crack. Despite the many times I made it clear in my boarding house that there were people there to help them— normal, similarly-aged girls—no one ever came knocking on my door. I took it so seriously that this almost hurt. I knew there were girls who needed help, one of whom was a thirteen-year-old girl with self-harm cuts all the way up her arm, with a new bandage appearing every week, but they were all too scared. And I know how suffocated they must have felt at times, because I felt like that, too, for a large portion of my time in England. So maybe I wanted to help them because it felt like I couldn't help myself and I needed some satisfaction of purpose.

As with most boarding schools, we got into trouble. We had a social centre on the school grounds called the Longy (goodness knows why it was called that, I still don't know—the Brits have funny names for all sorts of things), where we were given an allowance of alcohol once we turned sixteen (only beer, cider and wine). In my first term, we held a Halloween party at the Longy while I was still fifteen. The friend I had made in my house told me about a boy in our year that she could speak to, who could apparently get alcohol for us from downtown. So we all chipped in for a sizeable bottle of Russian vodka so that this disco would be made more manageable and we wouldn't have to resort to standing awkwardly in the corner for the whole night. Safe to say that it didn't take long before we were totally drunk.

What is also safe to say is that we all got caught, mainly because we were so oblivious to the world around us that we missed our curfew. We knew consequences were coming but we were unaware of how dire they would be. Mrs Swart caught me and didn't hold back—discipline from a housemistress from Rondebosch is an experience like no other. Without prompting anything as I was just going with the flow, and despite everyone conspiring to ensure we all told the same story, I received a Facebook message from the boy who bought the vodka for us, saying: "You bought the vodka. End of story. I wasn't caught and you have no proof. Pipe the fuck down and stop being so pathetic. If you rope me into this, you'll regret it. If you dob in on me, your whole year will hate you."

I was called in for my hearing with the head of discipline, Mrs Angus—one of the most delightful people, who is very difficult to dislike even though the future of my time at Malvern was ultimately in her hands—and told to tell my side of the story. I had forced myself to agree to speak the same as the other girls— that we bought the vodka and mixed it with juice and drank in our rooms before the party—but I evidently failed. Mrs Angus could see right through me and part of me was relieved as lying felt like eating away at the very essence of who I was as a person. I broke the seal and told her that another boy had bought the vodka for us, and had since then threatened me on Facebook. She asked me to show her the messages, which I did, and she seemed angrier with the other boy than at me for breaking the rules on drinking. Drinking on the school premises was a serious offence, but buying alcohol for another (I think he was older than us) was even more serious. Over and above that, she was angry that another student had intimidated me.

The cat was out of the bag and I had been honest, sticking to what I knew was right, even though it involved getting another student in trouble. I thought I had done the right thing. When I got back to my room and told my roommate what had just happened, despite the fact that she had no connection to the other boy whatsoever, she erupted. 'Snitching' on another student was the ultimate social crime, apparently. All the blood drained from my face.

She promptly went to tell all the other girls implicated in the drinking incident, and I was immediately ostracised. I was thrown back to that incident in Saudi, like one giant time warp, where I had been isolated for 'snitching'. I had been honest, a personal characteristic that I was, and still am, proud of, but this had been viewed as distasteful and as an act of betrayal of the student body. I then wondered who would befriend me for the remainder of my year and eight months left at Malvern College or if this would be a solo journey.

As if I didn't think it could get any worse, a girl in my house from the year above me barged into my room one day with a look of sheer anger on her face and rage in her eyes.

"How could you do that to him? How could you get him into so much trouble? Did you know he has been expelled and has to leave now? He was my friend and now I don't know when I'll get to see him again because of *you*."

I was stunned. I timidly tried to explain my situation, hands and voice shaking, but she refused to listen and didn't care. She was ruthless. She stormed out of my room almost as quickly as she had entered it.

A week later I went to town do some toiletry shopping, only to be followed back to my house by a group of taunting boys who stayed in the same boarding house as the boy who bought us the vodka. They were so close behind me that I could feel their breath on my neck, but I couldn't walk fast enough to gain any distance. I was relieved that they at least let me walk to the door of my boarding house in peace. Only then did my roommate realise the severity of how badly I had been targeted, and agreed to come with me to talk to our house assistant about it. I wonder why she had a change of heart given how furious she was when I told her I had leaked someone else's name.

The final school day arrived of the boy who bought us vodka. A girl from my house knocked on my door and told me there were people asking for me outside the back door. I looked out of a window and saw around twenty people apparently asking to talk to me about the boy's expulsion, wanting to hold me accountable and make me realise what I had done. What if I had gone out there? What would I have said to them? I was absolutely terrified—they were like an angry mob. I felt as if I would be walking up to the chopping block.

This incident pretty much prompted the beginning of my spiral into a deep unhappiness that I could only keep to myself. I couldn't talk to anyone about it because *not a single soul* understood me or where I came from, and I couldn't talk to my family about it because I had to reassure them that this decision to come to the UK was still a good one. The only person I felt vaguely comfortable talking to about my life was Mrs Adam, who turned out to be my saving grace. Mrs Swart and her welcoming home was also a huge source of comfort to me—my home away from home when I felt like I had absolutely nothing and absolutely no one.

I went totally silent following this. I tried to focus on the things I could control, like my soccer and my academics, and lived for leave-out weekends and half-terms. Any escape from the environment I was in would have sufficed. I felt like I was suffocating, not being with my family and true friends.

In my first semester at Malvern, I put on eight kilograms; by the following May I had lost all of it, and then some more. I was barely eating, partly because the food had gotten worse; I had been put on Concerta for my shocking concentration, and I was morbidly depressed. My grades went up which was fantastic, but that wasn't enough to keep me happy. I tried to get back into piano, my passion prior to soccer, which failed, and I disappointed my family and myself because of that. I was distant and angry all the time. But come any opportunity to drink, I was all of a sudden wide awake.

My friend from my boarding house and I would down our three drinks as fast as we could, in order to get as tipsy as possible as quickly as possible at the Longy. She may have taken part because she wanted to feel more relaxed—I was often criticised for being so uptight. I did it because I longed to feel confident in myself and my environment, and alcohol felt like the only gateway to this. We would smuggle in vodka in hip flasks. We got in trouble again on a school trip to Costa Rica where I was on my second strike and flirting with expulsion. The third strike almost came when I handed myself in for a mass incident of binge drinking at the Longy, but because I handed myself in it didn't go on my record and I didn't get expelled. This incident prompted the girls in my year to call a meeting in one of the girls' rooms to discuss how to get our stories straight if we were all called in. Everyone looked at me. The Halloween vodka incident had happened almost a year before, but I was still known as the snitch that everyone was worried about. Everyone was nervous about getting caught and they knew they could blame me if it came to that.

I didn't hide how furious and hurt I was following this informal gathering of fellow rebels. These girls had supposedly become sort-of friends as the year had gone on and our co-living became more cohesive. I was totally shattered from my head to my toes and my brain felt like it was going into electric shock. I was shaking and could not control myself.

I stormed up the stairs to my room and crumbled. I felt like a cornered wild animal let down by the very people who claimed they were on my side and would protect me. I didn't just cry, I sobbed, violently, on the floor of my room until the early hours of the morning. I then decided I was going to take things into my own hands and be done with this situation and my messy life once and for all. I had been prescribed Trepiline, an antidepressant, to counter the effects of the Concerta at night, so that I could sleep, and I decided I was going to take all the tablets I had left, that night. I knew nothing about suicide and what could kill me, but I knew I so strongly wanted to feel different, even if it was to feel nothing at all, at that point.

Luckily, what was left of my sane mind spoke to me in a whisper and I phoned my mom, who was fast asleep in Doha.

"Mom, I am so unhappy, and I want to die. I'm going to die."

I managed to mumble out some of the recent events, but my sobs felt like concrete blocks and I couldn't get the words out. I was due to go to the Loughborough University open day quite early the following morning, but right then I felt numb and immobile. Life at that point felt like a dragon I was forced to slay, even though I was dismally underequipped to fight it. I couldn't face getting into a car to see the university I thought was my dream— where I was later accepted to study English and sports science and could play serious soccer—never mind getting into my own bed. My mom somehow convinced me to still go, despite only having a few hours of sleep and possessed by a mind that wasn't my own. She told me later that ever since this incident she becomes paranoid whenever she receives a call from me in the early hours.

The days that followed involved me handing myself in for the third drinking incident, as mentioned, and also telling Mrs Angus that I thought I had a coping mechanism problem involving alcohol that needed to be seen to. I remember her responding with, "Wow," either because she was astounded that a girl so young could be introspective enough to identify such a serious problem on her own, or that a young girl like me could have a problem like this in the first place.

What followed was the appointment of the school counsellor whom I would see weekly. She was very sweet and incredibly kind and gentle, but I don't think she and I were a good match because, after most sessions, I still felt alone and misunderstood. I told her about the bullying, both in Saudi and in England, that had seemed incessant; that I felt like a ghost that still had to wade through masses of people every day despite feeling like breathing was a struggle; and that it had all become so heavy that dying appeared to be a much more peaceful option. That I wanted to swallow around fifty antidepressants regardless of whether they'd kill me or not—and do you know what she said?

"Um, Gabi, I don't think antidepressants can kill you."

Not: "Gabi, I am so sorry you think dying is an easier option here. So many people love you."

Or: "According to what I know, antidepressants can't kill you but the fact that you have these thoughts is a huge concern."

Nothing to let me know that I was not alone and that she was disturbed by the fact that *I wanted to die.* She sent no message to my parents or boarding house or anyone. Still, no one knew how I was feeling. I was convinced that I was walking the world alone as one incredibly sad, misunderstood individual.

***

One day, at the end of a visit to South Africa when my mom was dropping me at the airport to go back to England, I told her that she had almost lost me forever and *how would she manage if that had happened?* I know I had told her on the phone the night I had the intention, but I wanted her to know how serious I was. I broke down in tears because, just like the counsellor, it felt like she did not take me seriously. Anxiety and depression were not things she had really encountered throughout her life, so why would they now suddenly become defining factors in her eldest child's experience of the world? I could see she was in denial, which is normal and okay, but as a seventeen-year-old who so desperately wanted comfort and a defined place in the world, guided there by her parents, I felt so hopeless and so let down. It was her apparent unwillingness to understand what was going on that made me feel so sad.

But what exacerbated all of this is that I didn't really understand what was going on either.

CHAPTER EIGHT
Lonesome journey

What followed my almost-suicide was acceptance that I had to try to figure out what was going on. Defining the activity in my mind would then lead to a way forward, I told myself. But, because I had no answers to my snappiness, my anger and my argumentative, defensive behaviour, and because my family saw me as just being petulant, I felt like I was alone on my quest of self-discovery. I could still feel that my family were in denial about what was going on because I wasn't conforming to the usual 'put your head down and soldier on' approach that we, as a family, often advocated. I have to acknowledge that they were at just as much of a loss as I was, and I imagine they had feelings of hopelessness due to seeing their daughter unravel and not knowing how to tie the knot to make it stop. I was angry all the time and if this anger didn't scare those around me, it certainly scared me.

Alcohol was still an enormous source of comfort to me and our relationship became even more unhealthy. Although I had stopped getting drunk at school, I became excited by how much freedom I would have to drink whenever I came home to South Africa. I still chased after that numb feeling that drinking alcohol gave me so easily, because it felt like my brain housed a million furious, confused and hurt thoughts that held the rest of me hostage. When I came home for my end of term holidays, I stayed awake after everyone had gone to bed, and, although I'd already had one or two drinks with my family at dinner or in front of the TV, I would take a plastic cup (so that I could throw the evidence away) and fill it up with my mom's wine and take it to my room. One trip to the fridge would turn into three, and then I'd be drunk on my own in my room. I drank until I knew I could easily pass out, usually around two a.m., because the thought of sleep and trying to quiet my mind in order to fall asleep was utterly terrifying. I had lost control of my own thoughts. It was in those last few moments of being awake when my mind would wreak the most havoc and I'd wake up feeling like I had just fought a war.

And then I'd have to walk out of my room the next morning with a smile on my face, like everything was okay.

There was only one place in the world I always wanted to be, whether in Saudi or in the UK, and that was at home. In 2011, we moved into what was going to become our forever home in the KwaZulu-Natal Midlands, called 'Woodwind'. The idea was that my parents would die here and my future kids would be able to come here, too. It would be our meeting place when we were in trouble, in case we were scattered all over the world when my sister and I were older, and it very quickly became the place where we all felt at peace. You'd think, then, that Woodwind would be my ultimate escape from the toxic environment in which I was immersed in the UK. It was, in more ways than one, but it also gave me more liberty to suffer in silence. I would go to my room, ostensibly to go to bed after saying goodnight to my family. Darkness washed over me as soon as I was alone in my room and my headspace would change entirely. I suffered nightmares and night terrors, frequently waking up to see people with deformities in my room or to a breath on my face, unable to move or scream to fend them off. And I believed, for a long time, that my room was haunted. But it was really my own mind that was haunted by its own way of thinking. It was as though all the negativity and nightmares from my entire life were trapped inside me, and I was confronted by them in the form of these terrifying figments.

When I reflect on this, so many years later, I have to wonder if my brain is being selective. *Was everything really that bad?*

Because at that time in my life it felt like it was only possible for everything to be and feel bad, and I don't remember feeling true happiness for an extended period of time. Not that no good ever happened, but I couldn't have imagined looking at the world through glasses that were anything but dim and cracked. Even when I look at pictures of myself taken from this period, I can see how empty I was.

Because I spent much of my time on my own in the UK with the freedom to do so—upper sixth students enjoyed the privilege of their own rooms—I wanted the same at home, but this was difficult when you have a family that spends so much time together. I cherish this fact now, but back then I just wanted to be my morbid self without questions being asked. It was also particularly difficult because I still felt so misunderstood by my family. I ended up feeling torn between the desperate desire to be alone, but being afraid when I was eventually left with my own company because my rampant thoughts would then run their course uninterrupted and without distraction. Due to the fact that I found it difficult to be around my family (because of my own behaviour, too) and the risk of being alone, I lived for the end of December when my friends from Johannesburg came to visit for our annual New Year parties. When they were around, I felt like I belonged somewhere and that I was wanted, but this was a temporary fix for a deeply rooted problem, and, as soon as they left, I'd be back at square one. It was like a never-ending labyrinth of highs and lows, leaving me shattered at the end.

You may be wondering, after reading previous chapters, what my personal life was looking like at this stage. I was practically single for my two years at Malvern because the boys I met there were foul in comparison to my ideal boyfriend or anyone I had ever dated in the past. I had an on-off relationship with a boy back home, which existed mainly in my Twitter direct messages. He allowed me to talk about my sorrows and anger with the world, and although there was an element of authenticity about it, there was no future and I couldn't talk to my parents about him. Despite this, I derived a lot of comfort from him and I am still very thankful for what we had. I was also at a stage where I no longer wanted to talk to my family about my love life because they had heard enough in the preceding years. But this was also indicative of my headspace because I had never previously wanted to keep anything from my family.

There was a boy at Malvern who I met at the first Halloween party (where we all got drunk and were caught)—who was half-Swiss and half-South African— that I got along with really well and who I really liked. We went for a stroll together just before the party ended, and as we stood outside his boarding house, his hands around my waist, neither of us could pluck up the courage to kiss one another. We didn't get to see each other again except in passing moments on campus. And as soon as he discovered that I had leaked the name of the boy who bought us vodka-to Mrs Angus, he wanted nothing to do with me. (He had nothing to do with the situation except for being present at the same party.) He was the first nice boy who had even bothered to talk to me, so naturally I was disappointed.

My only other interaction was at another evening at the Longy, again well over my alcohol allowance, when I was dancing without much regard for what people thought of me. I somehow found myself dancing rather intimately with another boy and then had a 'fuck it' moment, despite all my insecurities and worries about what people thought of me, and I turned around and kissed him. We were then hooking up on the dance floor in front of my entire year, with some taking photos that circulated the following week. I knew the boy, thankfully, as he was in one of my Spanish classes and I thought he was nice enough. I anxiously waited for him to send me a message after our brief interlude even though we were both rather drunk, so I was excited to see an inbox from him on Facebook a few days later that said: 'Hey Gabs, how are you? You wanna chill today? Xx'

Wow! Even though he was so drunk that he had fallen into a bush, *he remembers what happened that night and now wants to meet up for something a bit more sober.* I was *so* nervous, but I felt flattered and wanted… until I found out from his friend that he wasn't the one who sent the message. His mate in his boarding house turned this whole thing into a joke. He actually had no intention of spending time with me after our very public evening at the Longy.

Then, that's exactly what I felt like—a joke. I felt embarrassed and belittled and I wasn't sure how I was going to face him in our next Spanish class. He was really nice and not quite as boisterous as the other boys, but what they all had in common was that they were cowards. They had enough confidence to kiss a girl and make her feel special for all of five minutes, often under the influence of something or other, but then didn't have the balls to talk to her thereafter.

Things started to improve in the last four or five months of my time in the UK—a situation not unlike that dreadful period in Saudi where things had just gotten better and then I had to leave. I still didn't have loads of close friends except for a girl in my boarding house and two others that I befriended in class, but I had started pushing back more to those in my boarding house who berated me and this helped me restore my power. I was generally getting on a lot better with everyone. Our boarding house was tumultuous at times, but somehow my year of girls managed to keep it together amongst ourselves. I became close friends with other girls on my floor, again considered the 'nerds' of the house, but who were unapologetically themselves and allowed me to be the same. I, at least, had someone across the corridor that got as excited about the new Fall Out Boy album as I did.

Mrs Adam continued to be my source of strength, and I one of hers when she went through a dreadful divorce. I had never cared so much for a teacher and the hurt she was experiencing and I wanted to be there for her, although I felt totally out of my depth with what she was facing. Similarly, Mrs Swart was my home away from home.

Towards the end, I had less desire to get blind drunk in an attempt to drown out all my demons because their voices weren't as loud any more, and instead channelled all my energy and focus into my final exams. In my free time I read books and spent time outside as I learned to love the English summers. And before the sports season ended and we all parted to start the process of preparation for end-of-year exams, I found family in my soccer team. We were goofy together on bus trips to away-games, and trusted each other. This was the only group of people where I felt I belonged.

I knew my time in the UK was coming to an end because, despite being accepted to all five of my UK university choices—one being Loughborough University which was rated highly—I had decided I wanted to return home. I wanted to be with my people and back in my country and so I decided on a Bachelor of Journalism at Rhodes University. Before I left the UK, I felt semi-healed from all the trauma. Although I had to accept that my anxiety and depressive episodes would come with me wherever I went—which they did when I started an internship at Al Jazeera in Doha before starting to study at Rhodes, and then while I was at Rhodes—I couldn't compare any new episodes to the ones I had experienced in Saudi and the UK as they were different in magnitude. And, if I were to combine the events in Saudi and in the UK, I would feel that I had lost a few years of my life that I could never get back.

CHAPTER NINE
Coming back to myself

Exams ended around May 2013, and I returned to Doha for a month to basically breathe and catch up with myself after two strenuous years of academics and living away from my family. At this point, my family were living in Doha, Qatar. My dad had a new job, so this was our base for the meantime. My IB exams had been nothing short of stressful, but I handled myself well. The most difficult part was waiting for the results. I needed to reach my expected number of points, which was thirty-five to forty-five, in order to feel I had done this journey in the UK justice. In the meantime, I made new friends in Doha through my sister, whose friends all had older siblings, and some of their parents had become friends with mine. Again, I joined a pool of people who were totally different to me with seemingly higher levels of life experience, even though we were all still teenagers. My anxiety was still prevalent at this point.

The release of my exam results was drawing nearer and I had become increasingly paranoid as I'd had two or three dreams that revealed below average marks. The day came and I read the transcript:

Thirty-one.

After all that hard work, the best I could do was thirty-one points? And my dreams told me I would get at least thirty-three. To say I was disappointed is an understatement, so I opted to have three of my exams re-marked. Two of them were successful, bringing my total to thirty-three—in line with my prophetic dream. I was a lot happier with this as, knowing the IB system, two points made a huge difference. And it was these results that secured me a formal acceptance into Loughborough University for English and sports science—one of the top ten universities in the UK. This knowledge alone made my heart burst with pride.

I later found out that the girl who was my first roommate and teased me to death about, amongst many other things, not taking science as a higher-level subject, got below thirty points and wasn't accepted into any of her universities of choice. This also gave me a small kick because of how horrible she could be and the huge role she had played in making my time in the UK pretty miserable. As I have said before, I do not wish dread and misery on people regardless of what they have done to me, but life does seem to have a way of dishing out karma in appropriate doses. Overall, my exam results, paired with my ability to semi-heal from all the trauma (amongst other accolades) made me realise that what felt like a gruelling two years was actually two of the most worthwhile years of my life.

In July 2013, we headed back to the UK as a family to attend my leavers' ball, which, to this day, is still the most extravagant event I have ever experienced. With red carpets, fireworks, French Champagne and a three-course meal, it simply cannot compare to the dances many have experienced in South Africa when leaving school. Unless you had a boyfriend or girlfriend, you attended this ball with your family and close ones. The other two tickets, aside from our four, went to my extended family who served as my guardians and hosted me in Tewkesbury during leave-out weekends. I was incredibly grateful to have had them there, and thought this was the least I could do to repay them. We trawled the malls in Doha in the months leading up to the ball, trying to find the perfect dress and shoes, eventually settling on a gorgeous red gown that fitted me perfectly. I felt like a real-life princess on the day, also thanks to my incredibly talented sister who did my hair and make up for me.

We all sat down to a formal dinner with our families in our boarding house's dining room, after which various awards were distributed. I wasn't expecting anything but I received the Sportswomen of the Year award, with my name engraved on the house cup, to be seen for many years to come. This felt like the perfect full stop to my time at Malvern. I gave Mrs Swart a huge hug as she handed the cup to me for a photograph.

I then proceeded to get disgustingly drunk.

What an ill match—a girl in a beautiful red dress, who had just been given an award, doing wine chugging competitions with her friends that she probably wouldn't see for many years to come.

I think all the travel had an effect, too, but it doesn't excuse the state I was in come midnight of that evening. I was vomiting in the bathrooms and could barely see through one eye, and my mom had to grab me by the arm and shove me in a taxi to be taken back to the hotel. I don't have very many regrets in life, but the way I threw away this night is certainly one of them. What I do remember is crying in the hotel room and asking for Mrs Adam because she was the only person I wanted to see, but she definitely wouldn't have felt the same if she had seen me.

Anyway, that was the last time Malvern would see me. I loved being glamorous just for a night, despite the way it ended.

***

I landed an amazing opportunity as an intern in Doha, at the headquarters of news channel, Al Jazeera—a dream for many aspiring journalists. So we returned to Doha, where I began preparing for my three-month internship behind their sports desk, thanks to my dad making contact with a connection he had at the network. Looking back, I seemed to have taken this opportunity very lightly and had no idea how monumental it was to be for me. For the first month I was incredibly bored and not at all stimulated, again allowing my nervousness and poor self-esteem to hold me back as I battled to put myself out there. An element of relief was that Robin Adams, a journalist from Cape Town (who, remarkably, started out as a bus driver), was at the same sports desk and we provided much comfort to each other as we remembered and reminisced about life back at home. Although I was bored with the environment initially, I was prompted by the executive producer to start a blog, which is where I discovered my passion for writing about socio-political issues in sport, primarily gender inequality in the industry. James Pratt, despite being an incredibly busy executive producer, provided an enormous amount of guidance and feedback in order to help me better my future journalistic self. For someone yet to study journalism, I accomplished a significant amount with my blog, interviewing inspiring people like Jos Dirkx, who founded an initiative in Cape Town that supported disadvantaged young girls who wanted to play sport, and Frans Hilton-Smith, the ex-head of women's football at the South African Football Association (SAFA). Similarly, for the rest of my time at Al Jazeera, I forged meaningful relationships with the other producers and presenters who genuinely wanted to help me learn. (I didn't find this at all at other internships I carried out thereafter.)

There was one specific day when both producers were unable to come in because they were sick, so it was just the presenter and me. She could not be both presenter and producer, so that's when I was forced to step up to the plate otherwise the bulletin would have had to be shortened, and compromised on quality. Basically, I was a producer for a day, and it was the most exhilarating experience I have ever had. This single day alone gave me a superb taste of what it was like to be in a newsroom, and I thought that I would love to have that kind of adrenaline as part of my everyday life.

I was a new person by the time the internship ended, and received an incredible reference letter from the executive producer. By the time I arrived at Rhodes to start at the journalism school, I was already miles ahead.

***

My time in the UK and my three-month internship made me a lot more academically advanced than my peers in South Africa, but I never once used this as a reason to isolate myself. Instead, I was constantly being reassured of my decision to move back to South Africa, to the run-down city of Grahamstown (now Makhanda), and to Rhodes University, one of the country's smallest universities. The people I met made my heart feel warm as I realised how much I had missed South Africans' humility, humour and accepting nature. Right down to their accents, I was so happy to be with people *who were like me.*

In my first year, I met someone amazing named Alex. He would later become my boyfriend, and I lost my virginity to him. He cherished who I was as a person and I hadn't yet met anyone who made me feel that way. He was the year above me, really good-looking (I never thought I'd end up with someone who had a muscular body because I didn't seem to attract that type, but there I was, staring at his biceps for inappropriately long periods of time), ridiculously smart, and with a soft sensitivity about him that I grew to adore. He became the love of my life and I thought we would be together forever. I breathed a sigh of relief because I had found someone who allowed me to be who I really was—who fell in love with me for who *I* was, and who understood, and carried on learning to understand, why I couldn't smile for days in a row for no particular reason, and why I sometimes felt sad with no basis behind these feelings. I didn't feel ashamed but I also didn't feel like he pitied me—he genuinely wanted me to go through the motions with him by my side, but primarily he wanted me to figure it out so that I could be happy. Simply put, he allowed me to feel all my emotions without influencing them. And he helped me understand what was going through my tumultuous mind and wanted to help me heal.

Alex's dad was a pastor. Consequently, he was an incredibly passionate lover of Christ—and this was all strange to me. I had not grown up in a religious household; my sister and I were just brought up to be good human beings based on what our parents had taught us. Of course, there are many overlaps between good people that live outside of the Christian framework and those within it. Even though we had this in common this was just the surface—there were many other mismatched ideals, like the way he wanted me to dress, how I indulged in alcohol, and how many times I said the F-word. Even though he claimed to love me for who I was, that he wouldn't push his Christian beliefs onto me but would rather let me travel the road on my own to figure out if it was for me or not, there were other parts of me he tried to mould into pieces that suited him. How could he take his agnostic girlfriend (who he had slept with) back to his incredibly loving, Christian home and pitch me to his family? How could he convince them that I was exactly the one for him, the woman he wanted to marry, when I was actually more on the opposite end of the spectrum?

I loved Alex with every fibre of my being but being with him caused a huge rift in my family because they could see the damage he was doing, and I couldn't. I essentially gave my family the middle finger because he was the one that I loved, and I would do anything for him, including sever relationships with the people that knew me and loved me best. It is only with hindsight that I realise that a relationship of this nature is not worth it.

Over two years into the relationship, my confidence and self-esteem were in tatters because I only ever measured myself against what he wanted me to be, and, if I was falling short, I did everything possible to make it up to him. My anxiety had come back in full force. I was exercising like a maniac to make sure I stayed in good shape for him, receiving comments from him when I missed an arms and ab workout or spinning class. I isolated myself from my friends a lot of the time. My holidays away from him were torture because I was conditioned to need him. All the time.

Come the start of my third year at Rhodes, in 2016, I noticed a change in his behaviour and the way he interacted with me. He was less sparky, less loving, and the more I noticed it the more I started to feel ill. He was pushing me away to prepare me for the end of us. He was in his final year and desperate to go overseas, although I always believed we were going to stay together regardless of our locations, but he told me that he couldn't do it. And because my anxiety had got worse and I relied on him so much to calm it, he implied that my heavy emotions were a burden to him and that he couldn't handle it any longer. I was holding him back and he said he needed to explore who he was and what he wanted in life, without me.

When he told me that the end of the first term of 2016 was going to be our last term together, I couldn't control my reaction because this was not part of my plan. Our plans. We were never meant to ever be without each other. I started shaking, I couldn't breathe, and I couldn't stop crying. But not an ounce of me wanted to be mad at him because I knew he'd somehow make me feel like it was my fault. I started to believe this, and I begged and begged him not to do this. I was terrified as he was so sure in his mind about his decision. I felt like I was being thrown away.

We agreed to be friends after our inevitable end, which seemed to work. We met up for coffee once a month (again, regulated and implemented by him), and I can't deny that hugging him goodbye after each time we met left me with a tennis ball-sized lump in my throat. I so desperately wanted to be with him but had to try to let him go. Even though I tried so hard to hide it, he knew I still needed him.

The breakup was the beginning of another ominously dark time for me. Before Alex told me that he wanted to end things, I told him that I was going to use the year to get to grips with what was going on with me, and that I was going to start seeing a therapist. I thought this would convince him that I would no longer be a heavy weight on him—like his mess to clean up—but clearly not. I did end up consulting a therapist anyway, which was one of the greatest decisions and experiences of my life and helped me to reconnect with my deeper, inner self that I had lost over the years. I also thought it was time to consider something more than my own coping mechanisms, so I went to a GP who put me on antidepressants and sleeping tablets. I can't say this remotely helped me, long-term, the way therapy did: I turned into a total zombie, couldn't go to lectures for days at a time, would stay in my bed for hours in darkness, and I struggled to genuinely connect with other people. Although the antidepressants helped keep me relatively stable, I still woke up every day in a dark, hazy cloud. Just two weeks into my course of antidepressants, I followed up with the GP who suggested I double the dose. My inner alarm system went off, which was confirmed by my mom, who strongly advised that I stayed on that course for six months to see how I went, before doubling the dose. This GP had a flippancy about him that was off-putting, and I didn't want to be regulated by chemicals. I was on antidepressants until the following year and then weaned myself off to go onto the more natural course of treatment, which was cannabis oil.

The five months that followed my breakup were a rollercoaster ride. As therapists will tell you, it is a little like experiencing a death where one goes through the various stages of grief. This felt like the closest I had come to feeling the death of someone special, except it was a *something* instead. It seemed as though Alex and I had died, and I accepted he didn't want to be with me and that he was moving on with his life. Knowing him, he had this ability to separate the emotional and the rational which I sometimes admired but which I, at the time, deeply hated. Did his loss of me not leave a void in his life as big as it would be in mine if the situations were reversed? And he had *chosen* to be without me. I questioned everything.

Although those months were up and down, there was a lot of good in them. I started a journey of discovering who I was without him, which was wildly liberating. There were days when I missed him intensely, but there were also days where I wished we were on opposite ends of the earth. And then there were days where I blamed him for a lot that was going on with me internally. Our breakup was the start of a string of panic attacks stemming from my anxiety, because I felt helpless and not in control of my life and emotions, because he had hurt me so badly and I could do nothing about it. But since these very same panic attacks have continued to lurk in my adult life, they obviously stemmed from a problem that was only exacerbated by him, not started by him.

No one can prepare you for heartbreak like that and no one is readily equipped to deal with it. You listen to nobody and you succumb to your weakest self. You will then rise the next day and feel indestructible. There is absolutely no measure. But then again, the wildest loves are not measured, either.

I met someone else at Rhodes halfway through 2016, named Greg, who I grew very fond of, who treated me well and had no personal ideals that he wanted me to conform to. My family really liked him and that was a bright green flag for me. We went on to date and took things slowly, until Alex found out and let me know he was devastated that I had moved on. Safe to say I was all kinds of confused because, if the opportunity had arisen before, I would have leapt back into Alex's arms like nothing had ever changed.

How could he make me feel bad for moving on? He told me he thought we may end up together again one day, which was stupendously unfair. How could I put my life on hold for—granted, he was the love of my life—someone who made no effort to let me know that he would love me and cherish me forever, no matter what? I was under the impression that he didn't want me but there he was, letting me know that he wanted me now that he knew I was someone else's. I realised his heartbreak then and felt terrible, but it is with hindsight that I realise how selfish and manipulative he was.

Because he had got under my skin and the very essence of my being, I began to second-guess the new relationship I had started. When I was with Greg, I thought of Alex. When I was alone, I thought of Alex. And lusted for Alex and missed him and loved him in every waking moment. I made some awful decisions that hurt not one of them, but both of them, when I went back to being with Alex—this time as a new, empowered person that had confidence and couldn't be controlled. But the resistance from my family was blindingly obvious and I couldn't sacrifice them again. We had just got back to being how we always were, and I would be throwing all that away. I couldn't do it. So I ended things with Alex after three months and went back to being with Greg. It was one glorious, steaming pile of mess. I struggle to think about it now because I am not a person who hurts others, but there I was hurting three people at once, myself included. And disappointing everyone watching this disaster unfold. I was impulsive and impatient, and I should've just stepped back and taken some time to understand what was going through my head and heart. Instead, I rushed into what felt the best at the time, only to realise once I was in it that I was being selfish. I am wholeheartedly apologetic and regretful that this happened.

Although it took some time to get Greg to trust me again, we ended up together again and lasted for two years in total. Alex and I cut ties entirely, but I still think of him. Often. I'm sure there's someone reading this who understands why.

Even though I ended up being with someone else, my relationship with Alex is still the one I reflect on the most. This is either because it was one of those first relationships where everything is felt deeply and all at once, or because he had me wrapped around his finger like an insecure sock puppet with loose threads everywhere. I think it was both, because Alex loved me fiercely and showed it, and it was this display of love that I chased for a long time afterwards. It's these kinds of first loves that imprint on you and leave you desperate and dry-mouthed when they end.

***

Although I was certain I was in a happier, healthier relationship, I was not happy or healthy in myself. I had picked up a huge amount of weight by the time fourth year of university arrived, and my headspace was like pinning the tail on a very confused, hyperactive donkey. I could see Greg was unsure of how to comfort me or help me and so opted for the frequently chosen option of sweeping everything under the rug. He was kind and definitely cared for me, and so we embarked on a long-distance relationship as he entered the working world in Durban and I began my final year of university. This started off really well and I was astounded by how easy it was to maintain a relationship with him, but of course it got difficult and the spark between us slowly dimmed. But we persevered.

I was so excited by my fourth year of study. I chose a digital media specialisation and was given the opportunity to be the Varsity Shield rugby tournament correspondent for Rhodes when Rhodes finally qualified for the first time in ten years. I was a real, practicing journalist learning real, practical skills that I totally took for granted at the time. What was more important, though, was that I had moved into 'digs' (a student house) with two other girls that were initially in the same university residence as me from first year to second year, and who were my friends and classmates during the times in between. They very quickly became my soul mates and I realised that, although we were in our final year of varsity and I had friends from first year and even from my childhood, people enter your life at the exact time that they are meant to. Hailey and Sam became my confidantes and loyal best friends and still are.

It was later on in 2017, when we moved in together, that I came to the conclusion that Hailey and Sam were sent by the universe, or whoever, to save my life. I thought my anxiety was bad in the years before 2017, but in this year, it reached an all-time high. There was another aspect to it that exacerbated my wobbly state of mind: my inability to handle alcohol. For a reason unbeknown to me at the time, I could not make it through pre-drinks without feeling out of control—if I made it out of the house and to the pub, at all. I was confused because I had no idea what was going on. Just the year before I was drinking way more than I was at that time, and had managed just fine. All of a sudden, three-quarters of a bottle of wine and I was paralytic. I then started having these strange bouts of fainting and light-headedness and decided it was time to see a doctor (unfortunately the same one who wanted to double my dose of antidepressants, as lovely as he seemed). I was also, strangely, eating a lot of ice and craving it all the time, and my one close friend said that it might be a sign of low iron levels. My doctor did a blood test and phoned me a week later to tell me that I was grossly anaemic and that, if I didn't get my iron levels up within the next month, he would insist on a blood transfusion. My friend was right.

The thought of a transfusion scared the living daylights out of me, so I swiftly purchased the very expensive iron supplements and breathed a sigh of a relief that I had figured out what was going on with me. I calmed down with the binge drinking until I felt more energetic and more confident that I could handle a night out. Things seemed to get better for a while.

Until one night, after a solid night of drinking, a dark part of my brain decided to overtake the good part and I lost all sense of who I was. My panic attacks, paired with the horrendous fainting (often in the middle of a busy club) had increased, and I felt out of touch with my body, brain and emotions. I felt like I was someone else's puppet and I had no control. Alcohol had eventually become a positive thing for me, after years of it being an obvious negative, even when it was in excess. But this night, it was not.

I was in the bathroom trying to make myself vomit from a night of too much booze, lying on the bathroom floor totally unable to move. I seemed to be looking at myself from the outside as two separate entities, because I felt entirely detached from who I was. I started kicking the door. Hailey and Sam scuttled around the house in confusion, unsure where the noise was coming from, worried it was an attempted burglary. They eventually discovered I was making the noise from the bathroom and picked me up off the floor as I shouted at them: "I want to die, and I'm going to die."

They put me into bed, and I convinced them I was fine—just drunk. I clearly had some control because it didn't stop me from swallowing approximately twenty-five painkillers.

Just like that time in the UK, my first instinct was to phone my mom. Then I phoned Greg. I told them both what I had done, and I don't remember their responses. I was completely disassociated from my real self. I was taken to the hospital where I eventually started puking everything out. Somehow, I still had enough sense of humour to speak to the doctor, who was Nigerian, about my Nigerian friend, Layla, from Saudi, and asked if they knew each other.

(*I mean, really, Gabi? You can be drunk and suicidal, but don't you* dare *be ignorant and conforming to stereotypes.*)

The nurses tried to give me charcoal to absorb the alcohol pooling in my belly but I refused, so they were obliged to note this down. I was put in a wheelchair and taken to a bed in a ward. It was only the next day that I discovered that my medical aid, which was a hospital plan, did not cover overdoses of this nature, so I was placed in the public ward. I was the only white girl there, with nothing but a drip and wearing my ex-boyfriend's T-shirt that I had to reveal when I went to bathroom to throw up some more. All eyes were on me, and it was *not* the attention I usually craved.

As the reality started to sink in, I grew terrified. I wasn't allowed my phone, I was dizzy and nauseous, I was confused and pumped to the brim with regret. Because my incident had happened over the weekend, there was a slimmer chance of a doctor coming in to check if I could be released, which meant there was a possibility I had to stay for two nights. But thankfully a doctor was available and came to ask me a few questions, to which I responded that this was a massive drunken mistake and I was not at risk of hurting myself again. During all of this, my mother booked a flight (not really something my parents wanted to spend money on at the time) to come to spend a few days with me and make sure her daughter was okay.

All I can remember is feeling stupid and embarrassed, but I have to understand that something similar had happened before. It was the same brain in my skull back then, the same brain that wanted to switch off. But I felt even more remorse for the damage I had done to the people that cared about me—I had sliced my family's hearts, including my grandparents', in half, and I would never forgive myself for that. Had I been successful, I would have been leaving a mountain of love behind. It was remarkably selfish.

My mom and I went to see my therapist together, when she was in town, which was really good for us. I subsequently saw him for another three months as we had found a loophole so that my medical aid would pay for the consultations. The sight of alcohol made me shudder for a while afterwards, but I slowly learned to respect it and its power and, subsequently, myself. My recovery took a while, but I eventually started to reconnect with who I was. I had to learn not to rush things.

I am still learning not to rush things.

EPILOGUE

It's always difficult, after writing a book like this, to decide where I am now. Have I come far? Have these experiences helped me to become better, stronger?

Did I ever really get over all the bad?

I don't think there's one answer. What I can say, though, is that this book was like self-therapy in the form of words and pages. There were nights when I'd end up in tears after writing a chapter, having to relive some of the things I went through and that I realised I hadn't totally recovered from. But there was also a heavy sense of nostalgia and catharsis with me throughout the process as I reminisced about such special memories and the extraordinary people that never left me. Remarkably, this book actually urged me to reconnect with a few people from Saudi, who I am in regular contact with now. I have realised with hindsight that their presence in my life was greater than I believed at the time. I recently spent two days with a dear friend in Cape Town, who I last saw in Saudi eleven years ago.

I am twenty-six, living in the ever-peaceful KwaZulu-Natal Midlands in our forever home with my family. I am in the happiest, most stable and loving relationship, and my family and I are closer than ever.

My sister and I are now best friends after a long time of feeling like there were oceans between us. I have phenomenal friends who double up as an amazing support system—we often remark that we are 'friends that are like family'. After finishing university, I landed a job as a social media manager and copywriter at a boutique agency, which turned out to be the best place I could have wished for to start my career. And so I entered the exhilarating world of digital marketing and quickly became a professional. After a year, in early 2019, I resigned to finish this book. The start of 2019 was also when I ended my relationship with Greg, after realising that we simply were not meant to be.

As it goes, things didn't go according to plan. I started a freelance business—to make some money to fund my book—which unexpectedly took off, taking up most of my time. I was then headhunted to work as an in-house content creator for a skincare brand, where I learned many more valuable lessons. Again, I knew there was something else demanding my attention, whispering in my ear often, so I left that job in early 2020 to freelance again and *finally* finish my book.

***

I still struggle with my mental health and have accepted my anxiety and depression are here for the long haul. I made the brave, but totally worthwhile decision, to place all my healing trust into cannabis oil, which was a discovery made by my grandmother who wanted my grandfather, then battling Parkinson's disease, to give it a try. And so my whole family gave it a try and we have never second-guessed our decision. My grandfather is a new person because of it, as am I.

However, this doesn't stop the demons from visiting every now and then. Over the years I have battled extreme depressive episodes and dabbled in self-harm, but my mind has a new ability to put things into perspective, to exercise control, to know when to take a step back and look at things from the outside. These episodes happen less often, and I have better control over how long they last. I have learned that it is important to let them happen naturally, but not to let them take over completely. It is difficult because there is this pressure that, at my age, you have to have a plan and, even if you do, these moments of darkness make you believe that your plans can be derailed at any moment. Thankfully, I realised that the demons whispering in my year seldomly told the truth about who I was and what kind of life I was destined to have.

It was also difficult bravely deciding to enter a new relationship when I still felt vulnerable and unsure if the other person would be okay with loving someone who wasn't all that together and whose emotions were scattered. I often felt like I had to explain how my anxious brain worked, and why there would be some days where I was sad for no specific reason, almost like a disclaimer. Instead, I should have put total faith in my boyfriend and my decision to be with him—if I felt like he wouldn't accept my flawed self, then we wouldn't be together.

All in all, my plans have been haywire except for the one constant of writing this book.

The dynamic in my family has changed for the better as my parents have a better understanding of issues not obvious to the eye—like mental illness—as they watched both myself and my sister acquaint ourselves with our anxiety. Kate's comes in a very different form and we have all concluded that it is not a one-size-fits-all kind of condition. My mom, who maintains that she has not changed since she was a teenager and that she can handle anything without letting it bash her down (which, to be fair, she can), has realised that she, too, has experienced anxiety she didn't previously recognise. When I was young, I felt like my mom was unapproachable about the things going on with me that I didn't quite understand, but now I can't fault her with the way she allows me to go through these hurdles with her unwavering support. I think it's partially because she now knows what's going on and why I experience waves of anxiety, as they happen to her, too. My mom and I are difficult to separate at times and our relationship is full of fun times and loyalty. My dad is always readily available with support, love and laughter, often during a very average game of golf.

As the writing of this book progressed, I realised that it is about way more than just my experiences in

Saudi. It became about a young girl trying to pinpoint her sense of self in capricious environments that made the process tricky, hindered by a series of bullying events and the difficulty I had in grappling with a traumatised mind that was inflicted upon me at a premature stage, and the long-term consequences of this. And then having to live with a mind that I felt I couldn't trust, because one moment it was thrilled with life and the next it wanted to switch off forever. Although these moments have become less volatile, I still have to accept that what I went through made a permanent impression on me and played an integral role in shaping who I was, and am now. These incidents will be with me forever, without a doubt, but it is my ability to reflect on them instead of wallowing in them that has revealed a strength I didn't have ten years ago.

It's not necessary to have lived in Saudi to feel like you can relate to some of my stories. These issues are universal, and my story is just one contribution to the conversation. They have made me more empathetic, less judgemental, and thoroughly committed to self-improvement and acceptance of who I am.

Journeys like this are no accident. I have to believe that. This book started as journal entries in December 2010. It has taken an entire decade, but I can finally say I did it.